D0984397

THE VISUAL TEXT OF
William Carlos Williams

THE VISUAL TEXT
OF William
Carlos
Williams

HENRY M. SAYRE

University of Illinois Press

URBANA AND CHICAGO

Excerpts from the following are reprinted by permission of
New Directions Publishing Corporation:
Collected Earlier Poems of William Carlos Williams,
copyright 1938 by New Directions Publishing Corporation;
Paterson, copyright 1946, 1948, 1949, 1951, © 1958 by
William Carlos Williams, © 1963 by Florence H. Williams;
Collected Later Poems of William Carlos Williams,
copyright 1944, 1948, 1949, 1950 by William Carlos
Williams;
Pictures from Brueghel and Other Poems, copyright 1949,
1951, 1952, 1953, 1954, © 1955, 1956, 1957, 1959, 1960,
© 1961 by William Carlos Williams;
I Wanted to Write a Poem, copyright 1958 by William Carlos
Williams, © 1977 by the Estate of Florence H. Williams;
Selected Letters of William Carlos Williams, copyright
© 1957 by William Carlos Williams;
A Recognizable Image: William Carlos Williams on Art &
Artists, copyright 1939, 1954, © 1962 by William Carlos
Williams, © 1964, 1974 by Florence H. Williams.

Previously unpublished material by William Carlos Williams,
copyright © 1983 by William Eric Williams and Paul H.
Williams. Used by permission of New Directions Publishing
Corporation, agents.

This book is printed on acid-free paper.

Library of Congress Cataloging in Publication Data

Sayre, Henry M., 1948–
    The visual text of William Carlos Williams.

    Includes index.
    1. Williams, William Carlos, 1883–1963—Criticism
and interpretation. 2. Visual poetry, American—History
and criticism. I. Title.
PS3545.I544Z878   1984   811'.52   83-1395
ISBN 0-252-01059-0

For Mom and Dad

ACKNOWLEDGMENTS

Various phases of this study were aided by grants from the American Council of Learned Societies, Wake Forest University, and the Oregon State University Foundation. Their help and generosity were most appreciated. Karl Gay and the staff of the Poetry Collection at the Lockwood Memorial Library, State University of New York at Buffalo, guided me through the Williams manuscripts there. Similarly, the librarians in the Beinecke Rare Book and Manuscript Library at Yale University offered me every possible assistance.

I would also like to thank a number of teachers, colleagues, and friends. I owe most to the late Arthur Oberg, who first believed in my ideas and then taught me the better part of what I know about reading modern poetry. I should like to think he would be proud of this book. Charles Altieri's acute criticisms and insights literally transformed my thinking. Donna Gerstenberger's unflagging encouragement and friendship made much of my work possible. Martha Banta, Berk Chappell, William Clamurro, Bob Frank, Dillon Johnston, Bill Moss, Fred Pfeil, Mark Sponenburgh, and Bill Wilson all provided more guidance and support than they can possibly know. The diligent research of Kirk McCombs saved me from many errors, some of which, I am afraid, I have probably reintroduced. Cheryl Watt typed the manuscript, more than once and sometimes in the most trying of circumstances, and for her patience and good grace I will always be grateful. I have also benefited immeasurably from the editorial assistance of both Richard L. Wentworth and Ann Lowry Weir at the University of Illinois Press. Finally, but for Laura, Robbie, and John I never would have written a word. They make everything possible.

CONTENTS

ILLUSTRATIONS

ABBREVIATIONS

The editions of Williams's work listed below are the definitive texts, as indicated in Emily Wallace, *A Bibliography of William Carlos Williams* (Middletown, Conn.: Wesleyan University Press, 1968), p. 3, except in the instance of *Paterson*. I have chosen to refer to the fifth printing of *Paterson*, which not only corrects earlier printer's errors but also differs significantly in its pagination from earlier printings. This later text supersedes the first edition.

A — *The Autobiography of William Carlos Williams*. New York: New Directions, 1967.

CEP — *The Collected Earlier Poems*. New York: New Directions, 1966.

CLP — *The Collected Later Poems*. Rev. ed. New York: New Directions, 1963.

I — *Imaginations: Kora in Hell, Spring and All, The Great American Novel, The Descent of Winter, A Novelette and Other Prose*. New York: New Directions, 1970.

IAG — *In the American Grain*. New York: New Directions, 1956.

IWWP — *I Wanted to Write a Poem*. Ed. Edith Heal. Boston: Beacon Press, 1967.

P — *Paterson*. Fifth printing. New York: New Directions, 1969.

PB — *Pictures from Brueghel and Other Poems*. New York: New Directions, 1962.

RI — *A Recognizable Image: William Carlos Williams on Art and Artists*. Ed. Bram Dijkstra. New York: New Directions, 1978.

SE   —*Selected Essays.* New York: New Directions, 1969.
SL   —*Selected Letters.* Ed. John C. Thirlwall. New York: McDowell, Obolensky, 1957.

Unpublished manuscript materials are referred to in the text as follows:

Buffalo MS—Poetry Collection, The Lockwood Memorial Library, State University of New York at Buffalo.
Yale MS —Collection of American Literature, Beinecke Rare Book and Manuscript Library, Yale University.

Introduction

In the summer of 1949, not yet a year after his legendary Blakean epiphanies, his arrest for robbery, and his subsequent committal to the New York State Psychiatric Hospital, a young Allen Ginsberg returned home to Paterson, New Jersey. His verse was still tightly formal, metrically regular, and fully rhymed; in this, at least, he was the inevitable product of a Columbia education. Soon after his homecoming he ventured across the Hudson one night to the Museum of Modern Art in order to hear a reading by Paterson's older and more formally innovative poet, William Carlos Williams. The reading excited Ginsberg almost to the point of distraction—"I ran backstage to accost you," he would confess to Williams, "but changed my mind, after waving at you, and ran off again." Although the frantic young man was too intimidated to talk to the elder poet directly, he nevertheless soon sat down to write him a long, adoring letter, which he sent off across town to Rutherford together with a batch of his more recent work. Ginsberg was most self-conscious about what he called the "old style of lyric machinery" in which he found himself formally entrapped: "I may need a new measure myself," he wrote to Williams, "but though I have a flair for your style I seldom dig exactly what you are doing with cadences, line length, sometimes syntax, etc., and cannot handle your work as a solid object—which properties I assume you rightly claim. I don't understand the measure. . . . But I would like to talk with you concretely on this." Williams liked the letter so much he asked Ginsberg if he might include it in

Paterson (*P,* 173–75),[1] and he invited the young man to drop by to discuss "the measure" as he felt the need.

Williams's motives for including Ginsberg's letter in his epic poem are complex—among other things, its sense of Williams as a positive influence balances the earlier, more negative letters from Marcia Nardi. But most important, I think, Ginsberg has instinctively located what for Williams was *Paterson*'s great flaw, its fundamental weakness: Ginsberg didn't understand the measure, but neither did Williams himself. In one of their "concrete" discussions of the matter a couple of years later, Williams admitted: "I don't even know if Paterson is poetry. I have no form, I just try to squeeze the lines up into pictures."[2]

Williams's discussions of his measure are notoriously inadequate. As John Hollander has put it: "Outside his poems, in his analytic and critical remarks about prosody in general, and his own metrical practice in particular, Williams can descend, in the rhetorical uneasiness and crankiness of the autodidact, to obfuscation at best and nonsense at worst."[3] Williams was sensitive to his failing. In 1955 he wrote another young poet who was interested in his theories and as confused about them as Ginsberg: "When it comes to your failure to be convinced by my recent strictures on the poetic line, forget the whole thing. . . . We are not even *near* a common enough agreement in the terms we are attempting to use to make us intelligible to each other."[4] The young poet this time was Robert Creeley, who was trying to connect Williams's measure to Charles Olson's notion of breath, an approach Williams had seemingly endorsed when he had excerpted a large chunk of Olson's "Projective Verse" in the last pages of his *Autobiography*.

Although most students of Williams's measure turn, with Creeley, to Olson's essay, the continuing inexplicability of Williams's prosodic practice is, I think, the result of trying to apply Olson's terms to a case which simply doesn't fit them. As Williams was finishing the *Autobiography* in 1950, he was groping for some way to explain his newly discovered form. Because Olson's measure was essentially oracular—and hence unchallengeable—Williams was able to adopt its fiction. "You may not agree with my ear," he wrote to Richard Eberhart in another infamous "explanation," "but that is the way I count the line" (*SL*, 327). The fiction that Williams was adopting—or, rather, the fiction that he couldn't let go—was the poet's sense of the poem as an auditory arrangement, a musical form. His lifelong attention to what he called the "American idiom," to the rhythms of American oral speech, in fact predisposed him to this kind of thinking. But by the time he recognized that this musical and aural explanation might not actually fit the case—by the time of *Paterson*, Book Five, and the *Pictures from Brueghel*—he had been weakened by a series of strokes and was no longer able fully to articulate his discovery of a form based on the eye and not the ear, the discovery of what I have come to call his "visual text."

But hint at it he did, not only in his subject matter—visual art: tapestries, paintings, and painters—but also in a number of scattered comments such as his remark to Ginsberg in 1952: "I just try to squeeze the lines up into pictures." He means literally up into a visual design, a recognizable pattern on a printed page which bears no relation to either sound or sense. It is *vision*, not sound, that the "variable foot" depends upon. And his form is arbitrary, imposed upon his subject matter, not organically derived from it.

If these seem large claims, that is only because Williams has been received by the tradition—by poets such as Olson, Creeley, Duncan, Ginsberg, and Levertov—as the aural innovator he simply is not. With Pound, Williams has been mistakenly canonized as a kind of father figure for an entire generation of poets who value speech over writing, performance over text, *parole* over *écriture*. In an interview with Creeley, William Spanos has set out this version of Williams and his heirs:

> Goddammit, what the epistemological stance of Williams and Pound and Olson and you and so many other younger contemporary poets generates is a poetry that is fundamentally "the *cry* of its occasion/ Part of the res itself and not about it." That's Wallace Stevens' phrase from "An Ordinary Evening in New Haven," but it applies *so* much more, it seems to me, to the kind of poetry that you're "writing," a poetry, that is to say, which has its "source" in the speech act as opposed to writing, as opposed to the poem as something you compose for the printed page.[5]

Williams's work, however, originates in sight, not sound, in a visual pattern against which the poem's aural dimension must assert itself. To leave the printed poem behind is indeed to fly off into "the res itself," into the American idiom, but it is also to sacrifice form.

The argument of this study goes against the "traditional" Williams. Its claim is that his last poems, the ones in which his new measure is finally achieved, are meant to be read, with the eye, on the page. The visual dimension of Williams's prosody has, furthermore, far-reaching epistemological implications. From the painters with whom he associated throughout his life, Williams learned one lesson especially: the advent of pattern or design in a work of art is a function of the imagination, and the justification for the artistic imagination is, in fact, its ability to order or compose its world.[6] The longer Williams wrote, the more thoroughly he defined pattern and design as visual properties which oppose themselves to a recalcitrant and disorderly world—a world which, in its turn, comes to be portrayed more and more often as a kind of Babel, a chaotic and fragmentary speech. In the simplest terms, the visual is the mind's dimension; the aural, the world's. In a fundamental sense, then, this study of the visual in Williams's poetry is meant first as a rebuttal to J. Hillis Miller's essay on Williams in *Poets of Reality,* probably the most influential reading of Williams's work to date. Miller insists that Williams's work embodies a "leap into things"—into what Spanos calls "the res itself"—which allows him to "give up the ego" and thereby to "give up also those dramas of the interchange of subject and object, self and world, which have long been central in Western philosophy and literature."[7] Kenneth Burke initiated this conception of Williams as "the master of the glimpse" in a 1922 review of *Sour Grapes.* According to Burke, Williams's obsession with "the thing upon which the eye alights" was a result of his "hatred of the idea in art," and with it "a complete disinterest in form."[8] I take it that both Miller and Burke see Williams as the kind of man that Nietzsche rather unflatteringly describes in his famous essay on metaphor, "On Truth and Falsity in Their Ultramoral Sense":

> Only by forgetting that primitive world of metaphors, only by the congelation and coagulation of an original mass of similes

and precepts pouring forth as a fiery liquid out of the primal faculty of human fancy, only by the invincible faith, that *this* sun, *this* window, *this* table is a truth in itself: in short, only by the fact that man forgets himself as subject, and what is more as an *artistically creating* subject: only by all this does he live with some repose, safety and consequence. If he were able to get out of the prison walls of this faith, even for an instant only, his "self-consciousness" would be destroyed at once.[9]

Williams, however, constantly resisted the "leap into things" of which Miller speaks—his faith in things was far from invincible. Conversely, he resisted equally the kind of leap into the mind or ego which a purely abstract art represents. Williams knew himself to be, for better or worse, an almost constantly *"artistically creating* subject." While he believed in the sun as sun, he also believed in the power of the human mind to metamorphose the sun. He knew, like Nietzsche and in Nietzsche's words, that

the "right perception"—which would mean the adequate expression of an object in the subject—is a nonentity full of contradictions: for between two utterly different spheres, as between subject and object, there is no causality, no accuracy, no expression, but at the utmost an *aesthetical* relation . . . a suggestive metamorphosis, a stammering translation into quite a distinct foreign language, for which purpose however there is needed at any rate an intermediate sphere, an intermediate force, freely composing and freely inventing.[10]

Williams thought of his poem as that intermediate sphere or force, the expression of an artist whose intellect "celebrates Its Saturnalia,"[11] and rejoices simply in remaking and redefining the aesthetic relation of man to his world.

Rather than giving up the dualism of subject and object which is so central to Western thought, Williams embraced it. His aesthetic was based on an unresolvable dialectical opposition: on the one hand was the mind, the imagination, and its potential to create order and form; on the other was the world, fragmented and chaotic. By the end of his career Williams had realized the futility of trying to achieve any synthesis of the two. He had become the perfect anti-Hegelian, giving thesis and antithesis more or less equal time but choosing neither. Not only would closing the argument between self and world resolve the interchange central to Western philosophy and literature, but the implication of his poetic effort is that without the interchange, and the ambiguity and tension upon which it rests, philosophy and literature would simply cease to be.

The "space" of Williams's poetry *is* both subjective and objective, but it is not a space created by any synthesis of the two. It is a space defined, on the one hand, by the poem's visual dimension, a dimension which embodies for Williams the artistically creating subject's imposition of formal design upon the world. On the other hand, it is a space defined by the variety and range—indeed, the ingenuity—of American speech. It is a space which not only represents the aesthetic relation between the artist and his world, but also embodies the relation between the artist and his audience. The poem is, as Nietzsche says, "the stammering translation" of the audience's speech into art, but not the kind of translation which transforms the audience's speech into some foreign language. Rather, it translates their speech into a foreign *environment*. Speech suddenly discovers itself in a visual mode. It becomes the "pigment" of the poem, as Williams put it in "The Last Turn" (1941), the "distressing" range of "detail" against which "rages the fury of/ our concepts" (*CLP*, 44). It is to this new poetic space, in which the demands of the aural and the visual unendingly compete, that I refer when I speak of the "visual text."

By the word "visual," furthermore, I want to imply two related things. First, I mean a visual experience in precisely the same way that a painting is a visual experience, something we encounter visually before we begin to "read" it. Second, I mean to indicate a kind of text which not only maintains the first kind of visual experience but also takes for its subject matter that very experience—the re-creation of a "Picture from Brueghel," for example. Because this second type of "visual text" is rather complex, including and extending the first, I shall suspend further discussion of it until the last chapter and concentrate, for the time being, on the first. At the most fundamental level, the experience of Williams's "visual text" is roughly analogous to the experience of a concrete poem. In the introduction to her unique anthology of concrete poetry, Mary Ellen Solt has said that, despite its variety, all concrete poetry must meet one "fundamental requirement": "concentration upon the physical material from which the poem or text is made." The concentration has several ramifications:

> Emotions and ideas are not the physical materials of poetry. If the artist were not a poet he might be moved by the same emotions and ideas to make a painting (if he were a painter), a piece of sculpture (if he were a sculptor), a musical composition (if he were a composer). Generally speaking the material of the concrete poem is language: words reduced to their elements of letters (to see) syllables (to hear). . . . The essential is *reduced language*. . . .
> In addition to his preoccupation with the reduction of language, the concrete poet is concerned with establishing his linguistic materials in a new relationship to space (the page or its equivalent) and/or to time (abandoning the old linear measure). Put another way this means the concrete poet is concerned with making an object to be perceived rather than read.[12]

Williams's "visual text" might be said to meet these requirements halfway. Though he does not radically alter the page, he does put his language in a new relationship to its space, and if he does not quite abandon linear measure, he does come to a "new measure." At the center of Williams's poetic is his conception of language as physical material; but this conception is by no means *reductive*, as it is for the concrete poet. And it is this sense that the materiality of language allows for the poem's flowering and its liberting *expansiveness* that distinguishes his visual text most thoroughly from the concrete poem. For Williams, the poem is an object to be perceived *and* read; the visual text does not dismiss "reading." The visual text is, rather, a dimension of the poem's experience which is parallel to its reading, an experience which in fact *completes* the poem.

As early as the editorial introduction to the fifth number of *Contact*, written at about the same time as "The Red Wheelbarrow," Williams emphasized the materiality of the poem, the physical reality of language: "'Subject matter,' so-called, as opposed to 'form,' an abstraction, is a distinction that does not exist in a work of art save as a division between types of material." Because words (as opposed to paint) inevitably possess subject matter does not mean that they cannot simultaneously partake of the abstraction of pure form. In fact, as Williams points out, modern painting merely stresses "abstraction as subject matter."[13] In an essay which appeared in the 1912 Blaue Reiter *Almanac*, "On the Question of Form," the painter Wassily Kandinsky asserted that "it makes *no difference whether the artist uses real or abstract forms.*" Once the artist "is freed from delineating a thing," whatever he paints "functions as a thing in itself." Kandinsky concludes that "pure abstraction makes use of things that lead a material existence just as pure realism does."[14] From this point of view the fact that words denote things is almost beside the point. As Williams says in his editorial, "the thing that has been said over and over again is that whatever the material . . . all in the work must relate to an intrinsic unity and not to anything outside itself."[15] This intrinsic unity—or, as he also calls it here, "the pure form of composition," "an abstraction"—takes precedence over everything else. If "all in the work" must relate to this purely abstract form, then the word, which also denotes a thing, must first partake of the same abstraction. This abstraction does not underlie and support a poem's meaning. Rather, it functions as a thing in itself, unifying and synthesizing the elements (words) of which it is composed, and in that unification it gives a new material existence to these purely realistic (i.e., purely denotative) words.

What Williams has in mind here is very close to the notion of "architecture" outlined by the cubist painter Juan Gris in "On the Possibilities of Painting" (1924). In a 1932 letter to Kay Boyle in which Williams constantly emphasizes the materiality of language, he asks: "Why do we not read more of Juan Gris? He knew these things in painting and wrote well of them" (*SL*, 130). "All architecture," Gris had written, "is construction, but not every construction is architecture. Before a construction, whether intellectual, material, visual or acoustic, can be architecture it must fulfill certain conditions." For Gris, "all constructions of the natural world" are "fine examples" of architecture:

When oxygen and hydrogen meet they combine in certain proportions to produce a certain quantity of new molecules, the quantity depending on the amount of each element introduced into the mixture, neither more nor less. Water can be produced synthetically which is identical both in quality and quantity with natural water. This is an example of chemical architecture, or real architecture, because the result of this mixture has a totally different unity, consistency and chemical proportions to those of the elements from which it is made. It has a new individuality. But the mixture of water and wine, for example, only produces a construction. The result has no new chemical properties, no unity, no consistency and no individuality. In short, it is not a synthesis.[16]

Let oxygen be abstract form and hydrogen be the reality of things, and this defines the architecture both Gris and Williams sought to achieve, for a time at least, in their respective paintings and poems. Since the writer's material, no matter how abstractly he conceives it, inevitably points to reality, the architecture of which Gris speaks is of the utmost consequence to a writer such as Williams, who was dedicated to the idea that art must possess abstract design. The idea that the abstract and the concrete, the subjective and the objective, could be synthesized to form a "new individuality" which transcends its constituent parts was attractive to Williams. But when he writes in his *Autobiography* that Juan Gris was *"at one time* my favorite painter" (A, 318, my emphasis), he is admitting that Gris's "architecture" no longer interests him as it once did. He had in fact accepted the notion that the marriage of abstraction and reality was a construction of "water and wine." Instead of synthesizing abstraction and reality, the subjective and the objective, Williams strove to discover a way to measure their interrelations, a way to record how each affects the other. In fact, he finally succeeded in writing poetry that both possessed the abstract design of a formal order and reflected the real disorder of his world, poetry in which the human mind and material reality were held in perpetual tension. His poetry did not synthesize the mind and the world; rather, it was the record of a conversation between them, statement and counterstatement, question and response. As Williams saw it, man was divorced from his world, and if the marriage Williams wished to realize in his poetry could not be made in heaven (no marriage ever was) it would nevertheless be a workable one. It would be a dialogue, give and take, that would make it possible at least for one partner to live with the other again—to bring them together, even, in a dance.

Williams's recognition of the divorce of man from his world, abstraction from reality, reaches to the very heart of modernist aesthetics. The divorce theme dominates his poetry until late in his career—until Book Five of *Paterson* was written in the middle 1950s. Until then, whenever the marriage he dreams of is realized, it is undercut by the isolation of its own accomplishment. Very early on, Williams knows the paradoxical nature of a marriage to the land and its things: the successes in making contact with the ground on which he walks, in his nature poems, for instance, are simultaneously failures to communicate with his people, a people with no sense of the ground at all. A 1926 letter to a young friend, John Riordan, indicates the aesthetic dimensions of the problem:

> I can't take a situation for what it is, that's why I was "dead" in the studio. I must look and digest, swallow and break up a situation inside myself before it can get to me. It is due to my wanting to encircle too much. It is due to my lack of pattern. . . . As I exist, omnivorous, everything I touch seems incomplete until I swallow, digest and make it a part of myself. I thank you for making this clear to me, you have been an invaluable friend.
>
> But my failure to work inside a pattern—a positive sin—the cause of my virtues. I cannot work inside a pattern because I can't find a pattern that will have me.[17]

Williams's problem is twofold: if he finds a pattern—as he does when he makes contact with the land—that pattern isolates him from his people and he is "dead" in his studio; if he accepts the "lack of pattern" which his confused people represent—as he does, "omnivorous"—then he cannot discover a pattern great enough to "encircle" both. His people are, in short, as much a part of his world as is the land itself. If he marries one, he is divorced from the other, a choice between the abstract pattern of his mind discovered in proximity to the land or the real chaos of his world discovered in proximity to his people.

In *Paterson* Williams would discover a pattern to "encircle" both the land and his people, but the split between them parallels a similar sense of divorce in the plastic arts which was not resolved until the rise of abstract expressionism, or action painting, in the United States after World War II. Kandinsky had recognized the split as early as the first Blaue Reiter Exhibition in 1911. At the exhibition Kandinsky chose to represent directions in modern art outside Germany by the works of only two artists: Robert Delaunay, whom he considered moving in a direction parallel to his own and whose work he called "total abstraction," and the Douanier, Henri Rousseau, whose neo-primitive work he called "total realism," which he defined in his 1912 essay "On the Question of Form" as the "simple ('inartistic') representation of a simple solid object."[18] Kandinsky saw "total abstraction" and "total realism" as the two poles of modern art, and he believed that they were irreconcilable as "ways" or styles:

> These two elements [abstraction and realism] have always existed in art. They have been classified as the "purely artistic" and the "objective." The first was expressed in the second while the second was serving the first. It was a fluid balance, which seemed to search for its ideal fruition in an absolute equilibrium.
>
> It seems that this ideal is no longer a goal today. The horizontal bar that held the two pans of the scale in balance seems to have vanished today; each pan intends to exist individually and independently. This breaking of the ideal scale also seems to people to be "anarchistic." . . . On the one hand, the diverting support of reality has been removed from the abstract, and viewers think they are floating. They say that art has lost its footing. On the other hand, the diverting idealization of the abstract (the "artistic" element) has been removed from the objective; and viewers feel nailed to the floor. They say that art has lost the ideal.[19]

Kandinsky turned out to be prophetic. His formulation goes so far toward defining the differences between the myriad "isms" and tendencies that developed in painting from 1910 to World War II that the German art historian Werner Haftmann has used it as the organizing principle of his mammoth two-volume study, *Painting in the Twentieth Century*. Haftmann points to "two symbolic acts of profound significance" which at once defined "the unconscious longings of the epoch" and the two opposite directions that modern art would follow between the wars, directions that Kandinsky predicted and Williams tried to reconcile:

> The first act was performed by Duchamp, when he chose an object at random and placed it in a strange environment as an image of the Other, whose accidental but very material presence invested it with the very unrealistic dignity of a magic thing, a fetish. In this act, the modern experience of the object was defined as the experience of the magical Other. The second act was performed by Malevich when, in order to define in the most rigorous manner the opposite of the world of natural appearance, he declared a black square on a white ground to be a painting. In this act, the modern experience of form was defined as the experience of a concrete reality, which belongs to the human mind alone, and in which the mind represents itself. The two acts . . . have nothing to do with "art": they were demonstrations, they marked off the frontiers of art at two opposite poles of human experience—the absolute thing and the absolute form, the reality of nature and the reality of man.[20]

Until World War II only cubism, the movement that began everything in the first place, attempted to integrate abstraction and realism in a single style, to establish the "absolute equilibrium" which Kandinsky claimed was "no longer a goal." The cubists seemingly shuttled between the two almost at will, transforming a bottle into an abstract cone or, conversely, a cone into a bottle. They qualified pure abstraction with realism and simple realism with abstraction. In their collages they championed the object, while at the same time they embraced Cézanne's famous dictum that "Nature must be treated in terms of the cylinder, the sphere, the cone." Kandinsky's formulation of the two irreconcilable modes of modern art is probably a subtle poke at cubism's unwillingness to "purify" itself by choosing one path or the other. But in its very unwillingness cubism laid the foundations for both paths, and from cubism both paths developed.

The issues raised by abstraction and realism, the tensions between them, can be seen most clearly in the apparent necessity the cubists felt never to choose one over the other. If Williams was finally unable to accept Gris's synthesis, he never rejected

Gris's sense that abstraction and realism should coexist. I dwell on the plastic arts and Williams's relation to them at such length not only to explain his sense of the "visual" in painting and poetry, but also to place his achievement in the context of a developing modernist aesthetic—from cubism to abstract expressionism—which involves, in turn, the development of a shift in modernism's focal point from Europe to the United States. Williams's career spans the modernist period almost exactly. It is at least the latent thesis of this book that the realization of a visual text in Williams's late poetry is to American poetry what Jackson Pollock's monumental drip canvases are to American painting. Both define the triumph of American art.

NOTES

1. All works by Williams are cited in the text by abbreviation and page number. For full bibliographical data, please consult the Abbreviations.

2. Allen Ginsberg, *Journals: Early Fifties Early Sixties,* ed. Gordon Ball (New York: Grove, 1977), p. 4.

3. John Hollander, *Vision and Resonance: Two Senses of Poetic Form* (New York: Oxford University Press, 1975), p. 5. Hollander's concluding chapter, "The Poem in the Eye," led me to see Williams's last poems anew. Curiously, Hollander himself concentrates on Williams's early work, particularly the title poem to *Spring and All,* where the visual dimension of Williams's prosody is more accidental and far less controlled than in his late poems.

4. Letter dated 3 February 1955, quoted in Paul Mariani, "'Fire of a Very Real Order': Creeley and Williams," *boundary 2* 6/7 (Spring/Fall 1978): 186.

5. William V. Spanos, "Talking with Robert Creeley," ibid., pp. 28–29. I have taken the liberty of normalizing the punctuation of Spanos's tapescript for the sake of clarity.

6. Williams's lifelong interest in and involvement with the arts has been widely discussed. The most important studies have been Bram Dijkstra's *The Hieroglyphics of a New Speech: Cubism, Stieglitz and the Early Poetry of William Carlos Williams* (Princeton: Princeton University Press, 1969); Dickran Tashjian's *Skyscraper Primitives: Dada and the American Avant-Garde 1910–1925* (Middletown, Conn.: Wesleyan University Press, 1975); and Tashjian's catalogue to the exhibition at the Whitney Museum of American Art, December 12, 1978–February 4, 1979, *William Carlos Williams and the American Scene 1920–1940* (New York: Whitney Museum, 1978). Dijkstra's

recent edition of Williams's writing on art, *A Recognizable Image,* is quite ample testimony to the wide range of Williams's interests. Needless to say, my own discussion of the place of the visual in Williams's work has been greatly facilitated by and relies heavily on the thoroughness of this earlier scholarship.

7. J. Hillis Miller, *Poets of Reality: Six Twentieth-Century Writers* (1965; reprint, New York: Atheneum, 1969), pp. 287–89. Most studies since 1965 have followed Miller. Dijkstra, for instance, argues that Williams is dedicated to portraying "the autonomous significance of the materials of the objective world" (*Hieroglyphics,* p. 145) and to this end attempts to rid his work of metaphor. In these terms, "The Red Wheelbarrow" becomes the classic metaphorless Williams poem—but it also happens to be one of the few which avoids metaphor. By Dijkstra's definition, then—and Miller's—Williams was mostly a failure. See, for example, Dijkstra's discussion of Williams's inability to suppress, in *Spring and All,* "his subjective interpretation of things seen" (*Hieroglyphics,* pp. 170–72).

To be fair to Miller, I doubt that he would himself make these same kinds of arguments about Williams's work today. My sense is that he would want to complicate Williams's poetics in the same way he has dealt with the poetics of Wallace Stevens in essays such as his "Theoretical and Atheoretical in Stevens," in *Wallace Stevens: A Celebration,* ed. Frank Doggett and Robert Buttel (Princeton: Princeton University Press, 1980), pp. 274–85. There he acknowledges that Stevens's work is generated by a play among three competing theories of poetry, only one of which is "the idea that the structure of the poem should correspond to the structure of reality." But as he says, "it is impossible to adopt one theory of poetry without being led, willy-nilly, to encounter the ambiguous inherence within it of the other two." That is, within the poetry of reality one can also detect the theory that poetry is an act of mind seeking to reveal itself and, more important, that it is a self-contained creation, the site of the interplay between the mind and reality wherein "the two change places continuously" (pp. 275, 280).

Another way of stating the thesis of my own study, then, is to say that it is an attempt to define the importance of this third theory to Williams's poetics. If at times I seem to ignore Williams's active engagement with the first theory—with the real world—that is because, especially after Miller, I hope I can take it for granted.

8. Kenneth Burke, "Heaven's First Law," *The Dial* 72 (February 1922): 197, 200.

9. *The Complete Works of Friedrich Nietzsche, Vol. II: Early Greek Philosophy & Other Essays,* trans. M. A. Mügge, ed. Oscar Levy (New York: Gordon Press, 1974), p. 184.

10. Ibid.

11. Ibid., p. 189.

12. *Concrete Poetry: A World View,* ed. Mary Ellen Solt (Bloomington: Indiana University Press, 1968), p. 7.

13. William Carlos Williams, "Glorious Weather," *Contact 5* (June 1923).

14. Wassily Kandinsky, "On the Question of Form," *The Blaue Reiter Almanac,* ed. Wassily Kandinsky and Franz Marc, trans. Henning Falkenstein, English language edition ed. Klaus Lankheit (New York: Viking, 1974), p. 168. If Williams did not know Kandinsky's formulation at first hand, he was undoubtedly acquainted with its gist. His acquaintance with the photographer Alfred Stieglitz almost guarantees it; see Dijkstra, *Hieroglyphics,* p. 17. See also Gail Levin, "Wassily Kandinsky and the American Avant-Garde," *Criticism* 21 (Fall 1979): 347–61.

15. Williams, "Glorious Weather."

16. Juan Gris, "On the Possibilities of Painting," in Daniel-Henry Kahnweiler, *Juan Gris: His Life and Work,* trans. Douglas Cooper (1947; rev. ed., New York: Abrams, 1969), p. 197.

17. Quoted in Reed Whittemore, *William Carlos Williams: Poet from Jersey* (Boston: Houghton Mifflin, 1975), p. 271.

18. Kandinsky, "On the Question of Form," p. 161.

19. Ibid., pp. 158–60.

20. Werner Haftmann, *Painting in the Twentieth Century,* trans. Ralph Manheim (New York: Praeger, 1965), I, 203. Though Williams was, of course, unaware of Haftmann's formulation, he was undoubtedly familiar with pronouncements similar to it, most unavoidably Eugene Jolas's efforts in the pages of *transition* during the 1920s and early 1930s to preach the synthesis of objective and subjective realities. Typical of Jolas's statements is his call, in an essay called "Notes on Reality" (*transition* 18 [November 1929]: 19–20), for a "new composition . . . conquering the dualism between the 'it' and the 'I' . . . produced by the balancing of the dynamic representations of the world with the spontaneous movement of the dream." Incidentally, "Notes on Reality" leads off a long section of *transition* 18 devoted to "The Synthetist Universe."

CHAPTER ONE

Formal Necessities

In April 1929, a young man named Richard Johns wrote William Carlos Williams to inform him of his intention to publish by the following January a new literary quarterly called *Pagany*. Since Johns had appropriated the name from Williams's 1928 *A Voyage to Pagany*, he felt he had to ask the poet's permission— and he wondered, further, if Williams might help the venture by contributing a manifesto, his service as associate editor, and "a good bit" of his work.[1] A somewhat skeptical but probably amused Williams agreed to all but official editorial responsibilities in July. Then, as he began to take Johns's project more seriously, he offered his unofficial editorial advice throughout the summer and fall; and finally, in November, he forwarded the manifesto itself, together with an essay entitled "The Work of Gertrude Stein." Originally Williams had thought that the Stein essay might serve as the manifesto proper; his working title had been "Manifesto: in the form of a criticism of the works of Gertrude Stein" (Yale MS). In the final essay he praised Stein for lifting writing to "a plane of almost abstract design" (*SE*, 119). Like her friends the painters, she recognized that "the purpose of art . . . lies in . . . its own comprehensive organization of materials" (*SE*, 120). For Stein, words and paint were equally materials waiting to be formed.

In an age of artistic manifestos it is not so surprising to find Williams subscribing to one. But it would have been at least something of a surprise to find a poet who is so often championed for his own simplicity of phrase and directness of observation championing, in his own "manifesto," the work of a

writer who is so often condemned for her obfuscation of sense
and opacity of vision. Williams went so far as to say, in the early
drafts of his essay, that "the vigorous and constantly augmented
writings of Gertrude Stein [are] in many ways of all American
literary works the most modern" (Yale MS). Perhaps recognizing the danger of aligning himself so intimately with the likes of
Stein, he dropped this sentence—and the title "Manifesto" with
it. The short manifesto which Johns finally printed calls simply
for a return "to the word," so that we might "rehabilitate our
thought and our lives"—still the point of the Stein essay, but
less radically put.[2]

Many of Williams's contemporaries might have agreed that
Stein's writing was indeed "the most modern" had Williams
printed the statement, but they would have done so only as they
bemoaned the fate of modernity. They would not, in short, have
agreed that Stein's writings were in any way "literary." When
they bothered to admit its presence at all, they regarded Stein's
"nonsense" as the symptom of a chaotic age which it was their
place to restore to order—as the disease itself, not as the means
for rehabilitation. T. S. Eliot would say of her writing, "It is not
improving, it is not amusing, it is not interesting, it is not good
for one's mind. . . . If this is the future, then the future is, as it
very likely is, a future of the barbarians. But this is the future in
which we ought not be interested."[3] Ezra Pound dismissed Stein,
with characteristic candor if uncharacteristic brevity, as simply
"old tub of guts."[4] Yvor Winters's *Primitivism and Decadence:
A Study of American Experimental Poetry* (1937) is even more
typical in that it ignores Stein altogether, despite the fact that
Winters's discussion is in part concerned with the debts of experimental poetry to French symbolism, and that six years earlier Edmund Wilson, in *Axel's Castle,* had established both Stein
and dada as the culmination of the symbolist desire to rescue
language from cliché. Winters's only nod in Stein's direction is
to establish a distinction between "experimental poetry" and
"pseudo-experimental poetry." Whereas the former "endeavors
to widen . . . experience, or to alter it, or to get away from it,
by establishing abnormal conventions," the latter "confuses tradition with convention, and . . . desiring to experiment, sees no

way to escape from or alter tradition save by the abandonment of form and of poetry." Winters mentions e e cummings as an example of a "pseudo-experimental" poet and never discusses the "type" again.[5]

In the same year that Winters thus chose to ignore radical experiments in literature, Williams championed them in an essay which would remain unpublished until 1954. From Williams's point of view, the work of artists like the dadaists and Stein revealed, perhaps more clearly than any other kind of art, what he called "the basis of faith in art." In a context that is strikingly antagonistic to New Critical attitudes he writes:

> The minute you let yourself be carried away by purely . . . "literary" reasoning without consulting the thing from which it grew, you've cut the life-giving artery and nothing ensues but rot.
>
> What we seem to be getting to is that all the arts have to come back to something.
>
> And that that thing is human need. When our manner of action becomes imbecilic we breed Dada, Gertrude Stein, surrealism. These things seem unrelated to any sort of sense UNTIL we look for the NEED of human beings. Examining that we find that these apparently irrelevant movements of art represent mind saving, even at moments of genius, soul saving, continents of security for the pestered and bedeviled spirit of man, bedeviled by the deadly, lying repetitiousness of doctrinaire formula worship which is the standard work of the day. ("The Basis of Faith in Art," SE, 178–79)

Gertrude Stein, dada, surrealism—and, though he does not mention it here, cubism—all answer a profound human need for Williams. They save the human mind from stagnation, and their ability to free man's imagination in this way is the basis of our faith in them. Purely "literary" reasoning, the kind of reasoning that Winters and the other New Critics championed, ignores the human need that provokes this kind of art—the anti-artistic world which surrounds us—and thereby severs art from man.

Williams was always able to speak of Stein, dada, surrealism, and cubism in the same breath because it seemed to him that they all agreed that to live in the twentieth century is to live in the midst of disorder. He sees in Stein's prose the embodiment of the century's chaos and confusion:

Stein's pages have become like the United States viewed from an airplane—the same senseless repetitions, the endless multiplications of toneless words, with these she had to work.

No use for Stein to fly to Paris and forget it. The thing, the United States, the unmitigated stupidity, the drab tediousness of the democracy, the overwhelming number of the offensively ignorant, the dull nerve—is there in the artist's mind and cannot be escaped by taking a ship. (*SE*, 119)

The kind of existence he believes Stein describes is the same existence he himself describes in the 1919 poem "The Dark Day": "interminable talking, talking/ of no consequence—patter, patter, patter" (*CEP*, 201). It is, as Williams writes elsewhere, what the dadaists call the *"Rien, rien, rien"* (*I*, 174) of modernity, a modernity epitomized by the age's most all-inclusive gesture, World War I. Stein's systematic "smashing" of language and dada's more or less random smashing of whatever it might meet are themselves gestures which mirror the war. Since "America is a bastard country where decomposition is the prevalent spectacle," Williams wrote in 1920, then America "should be able to profit" from the spectacle of dada, of a Stein. "But," he is quick to add, "the contour of America is not particularly dadaesque."[6]

What Williams means by this last statement is not altogether clear, but he is probably attempting to emphasize, in the context of America at least, the creative impulse behind dada and Stein rather than their destructive bent. Dada, he wrote in *The Great American Novel* (1923), is more than *"Rien, rien, rien"*—it is "the release of SOMETHING" (*I*, 174). The War had been, after all, a European affair. He had ended his essay on "The Work of Gertrude Stein" with the important reminder that "the purpose of art, so far as it has any, is not at least to copy" the senseless, toneless, tedious and dull stupidity of the country. Rather, its purpose rests in its ability to make "its own comprehensive organization of its materials" (*SE*, 120). The function of modern art, in short, is to order its disordered world. Williams shifts what he sees as the emphasis of dada and Stein, shifts his art away from decomposition—or destruction—and toward the "SOMETHING" which dada's *rien, rien, rien* releases, toward the rebuilding, the re-creation of his world.

In *En Avant Dada: A History of Dadaism* (1920), Richard Huelsenbeck writes that, on the one hand, dada "desires to be no more than an expression of the times . . . their breathless tempo, their skepticism . . . their weariness, the despair of a meaning or a 'truth.'" But on the other hand: "From the everyday events surrounding me (the big city, the Dada circus, crashing, screeching, steam whistles, house fronts, the smell of roast veal) . . . I become directly aware that I am alive, *I feel the form-giving force* behind the bustling of the clerk in the *Dresdner Bank* and the simple-minded erectness of the policeman."[7] Williams believed he had to discover and articulate this form-giving force behind the plurality of modern experience, and the formal design implicit in dada and Stein provided him with the first inklings of how he might manifest this sense of design in the poem itself. In her analysis of grammar Stein had discovered certain grammatical parallelisms which seem to transcend lexical distinction. In his famous essay "Poetry of Grammar and Grammar of Poetry," Roman Jakobson has noted a "remarkable analogy between the role of grammar in poetry and the painter's composition, based on a latent or patent geometrical order." For Jakobson, two word-sequences—*the farmer kills the duckling* and *the man takes the chick*—"fit precisely the same pattern . . . are really the same fundamental sentence, differing only in their material trappings."[8] This is precisely Williams's point in "To Have Done Nothing," the dadaist poem in *Spring and All* in which "nothing/ I have done" and "everything/ I have done" are "the same" (*CEP*, 247). Similarly, a cubist, given a stool and a coffee mug, would note that the two structures fit the same pattern, that they are fundamentally the same structures—that is, they are both cylindrical. But this revelation of abstract parallelism is not an end in itself; it is, rather, a means by which the different material trappings of painting or writing may be given a sense of unity. It is the means by which composition—as opposed to enumeration—is achieved. It is the device by which the *difference* between material things may be underplayed and, while never forsaking that difference, the similarity between them underscored. It is, in short, a device fundamental to metaphor.

One of the great heresies of Williams scholarship is the belief that Williams strived to rid his work of metaphor. Bram Dijkstra, for instance, praises Williams for his willingness "to give his poem over to the precise description of a single object," and J. Hillis Miller asserts that in "Williams' world there are no resonances or similarities between things, no basis for metaphor. . . . A primrose is just a primrose."[9] Both cite Williams's four flower poems—"Daisy," "Primrose," "Queen Anne's Lace," and "Great Mullen," from *Sour Grapes* (1921)—as evidence of this desire to forsake metaphor, for, as Williams later said of the poems, "Straight observation is used. . . . I thought of them as still lifes. I looked at the actual flowers as they grew" (*IWWP*, 35). But the poems themselves, despite Williams's disclaimer, are anything but "straight observation." They are founded on metaphor, on *subjective observation and interpretation,* and are in no way "straight." They are manifestly *compositions.*

When Williams was asked to contribute to Whit Burnett's 1942 anthology *This Is My Best,* these are the four poems he chose. Introducing them for the anthology, Williams wrote:

> In the forms of the arts many things get locked up, some of them permanent and valuable and some of them stultifying if allowed to remain fixed. Unless every age claims the world for its own and makes it so by its own efforts in its own day and unless the mark of this effort is left upon all the forms of that age including those formal expressions which we call art, no one can be said to have lived.[10]

Thus Williams's flowers are emblems of his age's plurality: the daisy is the "dayseye," a man, a woman, a "limpid seashell" (*CEP*, 208); the primrose is "a disinclination to be . . . a rose":

It is summer!
It is the wind on a willow,
the lap of waves, the shadow
under a bush, a bird, a bluebird
three herons, a dead hawk
rotting on a pole—

. . . .

It is a piece of blue paper
in the grass or a threecluster of

>   green walnuts swaying, children
>   playing croquet or one boy
>   fishing, a man
>   swinging his pink fists
>   as he walks—
>   (CEP, 209)

The primrose seems to be, in short, everything in summer but a
rose and itself. "Each flower" in a field of Queen Anne's lace is
"a hand's span" of a woman's "whiteness," and each of the
woman's parts is a single "blossom under his touch/ to which
the fibre of her being/ stem one by one." Her body is composed
of each "single stem" which joins in "a cluster, flower by flower,"
finally to compose "the whole field" (CEP, 210). Great Mullen
is a lighthouse, "a mast with a lantern," "cowdung," "birdlime
on a fencerail," the man who has cuckolded the poet, and the
poet himself (CEP, 211).

   In these poems Williams has turned the function of metaphor
around on itself: where metaphor is generally considered to be
a means of evoking and defining the image—pinning down the
flower, in this case—the image now becomes at once the nexus
and generator of a whole range of metaphors. It organizes the
various materials of modern experience around itself. Williams
has not rid his work of metaphor; rather, he has reconceived
metaphor, freed it. Metaphor is no longer one of those "forms"
in which "many things get locked up . . . some of them stultifying if allowed to remain fixed." "The rose is obsolete" for
Williams, in another flower poem, because of the stultifying
metaphoric "burden" it has been asked to carry ("The Rose,"
CEP, 249), a burden Williams elsewhere overturns in a bald
parody of Robert Burns:

>   My luv
>   is like
>   a
>   greenglass insulator
>   on
>   a blue sky[11]

On the one hand, this is a startlingly direct piece of observation—a "straight" vision of the kind of telephone or power-line

insulator that is today a collector's item. But on the other hand, as a rather complicated metaphor (love as insulator as rose), it is a remarkable imaginative achievement—at once a funny and a scathing indictment of both love and verse. It is preeminently an example of an act of mind freeing the rose as image and opening it to possibility, as the rose in the other, more famous poem "unbruised/ penetrates space" (*CEP*, 250).

The four "flower poems" and the rose poem were written just as surrealism—the movement which longed to dissolve the distinction between the imaginary and the real once and for all—was taking hold in Europe, and they suggest, like surrealism, that most of our traditional poetic resources are empty. Williams's poetic mode here is, in fact, very similar to the surrealists'. His metaphors, because of their plurality and audacity, are just as extravagant, an extravagance designed to challenge the formulaic way in which we normally see our world. Writing in 1938 on the subject of surrealist metaphor, Williams in fact defines his own practice in these poems: "By retaining a firmness of extraordinary word juxtapositions while dealing wholly with a world with which the usual mind is unfamiliar a counterfoil to the vague and excessively stupid juxtapositions commonly known as 'reality' is created."[12] Also like the surrealists, Williams emphasizes the erotic content of his material, transforming the Great Mullen into a phallic symbol and the field of Queen Anne's lace into a woman's body. While the daisy is referred to by the masculine pronoun ("he"), Williams is careful to say, in a gesture which destroys antinomies in a typically casual surrealist fashion, that the flower "is a woman also." In all four flower poems his diction combines the formal and the colloquial. His tone, especially in "Great Mullen," fuses the high with the low, the refined with the base: "I am a point of dew on a grass-stem" alongside "You are cowdung." And the formal structure of the flower poems, especially the syntactical repetition of "Primrose," matches the "secular litanic" form so often found in the surrealists' work. Finally, Williams, like the surrealists, transforms his world in these poems. Our willingness to read the four poems he considered his best in 1942 as "flower poems" is testimony enough to his success. Not one of Williams's four "flowers" is, after all, a garden flower. All are weeds—wild and unruly— which, in the act of the poem, Williams cultivates.[13]

Surrealist attitudes and techniques—or notions similar to them—abound in Williams's work, and his attraction to surrealism is evident in the very existence of his 1929 translation of Philippe Soupault's *Last Nights of Paris*, a bizarre, dreamlike, and illogical account of a French prostitute who wanders through the Paris nights, turning the city into a labyrinthine and senseless (though undeniably sensual) hell. In *I Wanted to Write a Poem*, Williams calls both *Kora in Hell* and *A Novelette* examples of "automatic writing" (*IWWP*, 49); and he must have in mind the kind of writing generated by Soupault's and Breton's "psychic automatism." Williams's writing is close enough to surrealism that, when the French surrealists migrated to New York in 1941 in order to escape World War II, he was asked to co-edit with Breton the surrealist publication *VVV*. He declined the offer, despite the fact that he was sympathetic to the surrealist project. "Don't kick at the surrealists," he wrote in a 1944 manuscript called "The Visitors." "Of course they are frustrated. Who isn't? But! they are not frustrated when they write, paint, carve. That's the thing that concerns the artist. They, digging out a non-frustration, put their work into actuality, producing the distinct outlines of defeat in actual words, colors, contours. By that they are pure artists in the true tradition of their various professions" (*RI*, 221). Williams would go so far as to say, in an essay that he hoped would initiate an American magazine with surrealist ties, that both surrealism and "thought and effort in America" shared "the Midas touch, the alchemy of the mind which cannot be seduced by political urgencies—but makes all into gold."[14]

But if Williams was sympathetic to the surrealist venture, he was antagonistic as well. Both his enthusiasm for and his reservations about the movement could in fact be extended to most other modern art, including his own. In "The Visitors" he complained that the surrealists seemed "degenerate, insane and worst of all tiresome." And if he was willing to admit that "they, in their abasement, may well prove the means to lead . . . through to the light" (*RI*, 221), as the dadaists' *rien, rien, rien* had itself created *something*, he also believed that the surrealists had turned their back on "what is found in life" (*SE*, 252) and concentrated instead on the portrayal of the artist's imagination to the exclusion of material reality. In this way, he felt, surrealism failed "to communicate with people" (*SE*, 252). Similarly, what Williams valued in Gertrude Stein's work was her recognition of the importance of abstraction to writing. From her point of view, it was only in the creation of an abstract design or pattern that the imagination could reveal itself, and Williams agreed. The problem with her writing, Williams felt, was that in its identification of the imagination with total abstraction, the imagination lost contact with the world. He recognized this as early as his own *Kora in Hell: Improvisations,* the subtitle of which he probably derived from Kandinsky's series of abstract paintings of the same title. (Kandinsky had said that an "improvisation" is the "largely unconscious, spontaneous expression of inner character, non-material nature."[15]) Williams comments on one of his own more opaque improvisations: "It is obvious that if in flying an airplane one reached such an altitude that all sense of direction and every intelligible perception of the world were lost there would be nothing left to do but to come down to that point at which eyes regained their power" (*I*, 79). As in most of the more interesting modern art, "the virtue of the improvisations is their placement in a world of new values," he wrote in *Spring and All,* "their fault is their dislocation of sense, often complete" (*I*, 116–17). And in *The Great American Novel* he comments, in a moment of despair, that his work is "Joyce with a difference. The difference being greater opacity, less erudition, reduced power of perception . . . a ridiculous extreme. No excuse for this sort of thing. Amounts to a total occlusion of intelligence. Substitution of something else. What? Well, nonsense. Since you drive me to it" (*I*, 167). Any painting or writing which leaves the objective world behind and envelops itself in its own subjectivity risks becoming "nonsense." As late as the 1950s Williams continued to insist on the importance of the representational and the descriptive to painting and writing:

> Modern painters . . . have been afraid of the horrible word "representational"; they have run screaming into the abstract, forgetting that all painting is representational, even the most abstract,

the most subjective, the most distorted. The only question that can present itself is: What do you choose to represent? . . . For a while the painters chose to paint "subjectively." Influenced by Freud they discovered the subconscious and represented it on their canvases. . . . The subjectivist field has been exhausted . . . it was a mere sidepocket. (*RI,* 197–98)

Desiring to open us to the reality of imagination, the surrealists, Stein, the cubists at their most hermetic, and Williams himself in a work like *Kora* neglected the reality of the world. Their mistake would, in turn, become the mistake of American abstract expressionism. Jackson Pollock's work, Williams wrote, suffers from "the Sigmund Freud disease. . . . It is the record of a terrific struggle on the artist's part to reestablish in the face of a universal schizophrenia, a split personality, or more comprehensively, a fractured personality." All of these manifestations of pure subjectivity in the arts "represent to the eye . . . an incompleteness, a partial development" (*RI,* 206). For Williams, they could only hope to complete themselves, to develop fully, in the return to objective reality. As he wrote in a 1945 review of Karl Shapiro's poetry, it is "all right" to "use words as pigments," but Shapiro is correct in putting "a quietus on the 'abstractionists' so far as writing (with words) is concerned" when he writes:

> No conception
> Too far removed from literal position
> Can keep its body.
> (*SE,* 260)

The abstract "conception" must manifest itself in a concrete "body." Abstraction must "come down to that point" where it can be understood; it must, to borrow the name of one of Williams's earliest little magazines, make "contact" with the real.

II

Juan Gris was Williams's favorite painter throughout the 1920s and into the 1930s because he so consistently brought his art "down to that point" where it could make contact with reality.

There is a 1921 letter from Gris to Amédée Ozenfant, the French critic and painter whose purist school of painting championed the return to the object which it witnessed in Gris's synthetic cubism:

> Two outstanding works of art, whose importance is beyond question, have come down to us—the Venus of Milo, which represents Greece, and the Mona Lisa, which represents the Renaissance. They strike us with greater force than other works of art of the same periods because they have more individuality. The Venus of Milo has no arms—an individual characteristic. Now what is more potent than this act of natural selection as an argument against a form of art which confines itself to idealism and abstraction and refuses to become worldly and temporal.[16]

In "The Possibilities of Painting" he further explained the necessity for giving abstract thought concrete body by noting that it was the only way to guarantee a proper response to one's work of art.

> Why need one give these [abstract] forms the significance of reality, since a harmony already exists between them and they have an architectural unity? To which I would reply: The power of suggestion in every painting is considerable. Every spectator tends to ascribe his own subject to it. One must foresee, anticipate and ratify this suggestion, which will inevitably occur, by transforming into a subject this abstraction, this architecture which is solely the result of pictorial technique. Therefore the painter must be his own spectator and must modify the appearance of the relationships between the abstract forms.[17]

Thus, in the 1926 *Dish of Pears,* which appeared untitled in *transition* 1 (May 1927), Gris particularizes the abstract design of his canvas by means of three dark lines which delineate the base of the dish itself and outline the fruit therein. The abstract forms of the canvas could be nearly meaningless—a pattern of overlapping planes and no more—save for these lines. If we take Gris at his word, these lines were added last:

> I work with the elements of the intellect, with the imagination. I try to make concrete that which is abstract. I proceed from the general to the particular, by which I mean I start with an abstrac-

Juan Gris. *Dish of Pears.* 1926. Oil on canvas, 10⅝ x 13¾". Collection unknown.

tion in order to arrive at a true fact. Mine is an art of synthesis, of deduction. . . .

I want to arrive at a new specification; starting from a general type I want to make something particular and individual.[18]

The three dark lines which form the fruit and the dish bring the painting's abstract design to a representational and particular subject matter.

Despite the fact that Williams felt capable of a kind of abstraction—in *Kora in Hell*, for instance—which would require the kind of return to objective reality which Gris describes, the problem that tormented him most as a writer was quite the opposite of Gris's. We approach the painter's and the writer's media differently. If Gris could draw a design—a curved line, for example—which we accept as free of denotation, Williams could hardly write a word which would be similarly free. Before he would need to bother to retrieve for language its connection to objective reality, which is, after all, taken for granted, he had to establish some consistent sense of language's abstract side. Williams thus championed any art which contributed to his understanding of abstraction—from Stein's to Pollock's. He shared with Kandinsky's expressionism, with cubism, and with surrealism a sense that in the abstract lay a revelation of order which might unify the chaos of modernity. His work is the record of a constant effort to discover a place for abstraction in his poetry— an effort complicated, however, by his honesty: his realization that the order discovered in most modern work is one independent of objective reality, rather than one integrally related to it in any organic sense.[19] Thus his poetry is torn by two seemingly contradictory allegiances: he believes in the necessity of order, the design of abstraction, but he will not deny the multiplicity and chaos of experience merely to satisfy this necessity.

In *Kora in Hell* Williams outlined two different ways in which the imagination serves the poet. The *Improvisations* themselves concentrate on the ability of the imagination to go "from one thing to another" (*I*, 14), its ability to accommodate itself to the multiplicity of reality which surrounds it. But as the commentaries on the *Improvisations* proper indicate by their very presence, he knew that he must also *design* this random leaping about: "design is a function of the IMAGINATION," he would write in *Spring and All* (*I*, 98), and we measure a poem's worth, he writes in the Prologue to *Kora in Hell*, "by no quality it borrows from a logical recital of events nor from the events themselves but solely from that attenuated power which draws perhaps many broken things into a dance giving them thus a full being" (*I*, 16–17). This idea of a design which stands above material reality and forms it, a design which represents the imagination, is the same idea of formal design which abstract artists such as Malevich regarded (to borrow Werner Haftmann's phrase) as "the modern experience of form . . . the experience of a concrete reality, which belongs to the human mind alone, and in which the mind represents itself."[20] Williams would articulate this effort to realize abstract form in the poem most satisfactorily in his 1944 "Writer's Prologue to a Play in Verse" (*CLP*, 12, my emphasis):

> In your minds you jump from doors
> to sad departings, pigeons, dreams
> of terror, to cathedrals.
>
> .   .   .   .
>
>   You see it
> in your minds and the mind at once
> jostles it, turns it about, examines
> and arranges it to suit its fancy.
> *Or rather changes it after a pattern*
> *which is the mind itself,* turning
> and twisting the theme until it gets
> a meaning or finds no meaning and
> is dropped. By such composition,
> without code, the scenes we see move
> and, as it may happen, make
> a music, a poetry
> which the poor poet copies if
> and only if he is able.

This is the articulation of an effort to capture "a music, a poetry," "a pattern which is the mind itself" independent of the multiplicity of reality that is clearly begun at the time of *Kora in Hell* and "Primrose."

In "Primrose" the complexity of Williams's metaphor is sustained by the pattern of repetition of the simple phrase "It is" throughout the poem. Many of Williams's longer poems from 1918 on depend upon similar repetitive structures—syntactic and/or typographical—to unify the diverse elements of which they are composed. In *A Novelette,* written during the great flu epidemic of the mid-1920s though not published until 1932, he would call this revelation of the formal relationships among things "conversation as design" (*I*, 286), the relationships themselves being the "conversation" among things which formal repetitions reveal as "design." "Conversation as design" is the revelation of the "singleness I see in everything" (*I*, 283), what he calls "the simplicity of disorder" (*I*, 275). The revelation of an abstract design unifies the disorder and multiplicity of the world. In a long conversation with his wife, Williams explicitly ties this idea to the painting and drawing of Juan Gris:

> Always the one thing in Juan Gris. Conversation as design. . . . That would be writing.
>
> What's that?
>
> In which conversation was actual to the extent that it would be pure design. . . . It is the one thing I admire in his drawings—since there is nothing else. . . . Conversation of which there is none in novels and the news.
>
> Oh, yes, there is.
>
> Oh, no, there is not. It is something else. To be conversation, it must have no other purpose than the roundness and the color and the repetition of grapes in a bunch, such grapes as those of Juan Gris which are related more to a ship at sea than to the human tongue. As they are.
>
> The singleness of Juan Gris. . . . pure design—like the paintings of Juan Gris. (*I*, 286–88)[21]

The grapes Williams discusses here are probably the same grapes which occur in Gris's synthetic work *The Open Window* (1921), which Williams describes more fully in *Spring and All:*

> Here is a shutter, a bunch of grapes, a sheet of music, a picture of sea and mountains (particularly fine) which the onlooker is not for a moment permitted to witness as an "illusion." One thing laps over on the other, the cloud laps over on the shutter, the

Juan Gris. *The Open Window.* 1921. Oil on canvas, 25¾ x 39½″. Collection M. Meyer-Mahler, Zurich.

bunch of grapes is part of the handle of the guitar, the mountain and sea are obviously not "the mountain and sea," but a picture of the mountain and the sea. All drawn with admirable simplicity and excellent design—all a unity—[22] (*I*, 110–11)

By not permitting us to look at the things in this painting as "illusion," in the simplicity of their presentation Gris draws our attention to the imagination which has designed them. In the careful design of the canvas, especially in the subtle repetition of forms, colors, and patterns, the mind at work is revealed.

Gris's pattern of repetition in *The Open Window* would be adapted by Williams to his own poetic efforts. Williams wanted to reveal the same unity and design in the "conversation" among things—their *rapport,* as Gris called it. Gris organized the things in the canvas by means of an overlying abstract design, in response to the fragmentation and multiplicity which had marked the analytic cubism of Picasso and Braque. As early as 1915 Gris had written his friend D.-H. Kahnweiler that "my pictures begin to have a unity which they have lacked till now. They are no longer the inventories of objects which used to depress me so much."[23] In 1921, the same year when he painted *The Open Window,* he would conclude in the now-famous statement for *L'Esprit Nouveau* which gave synthetic cubism its name, that "this painting is to the other [i.e., the analytic cubism of Picasso and Braque] what poetry is to prose."[24]

For Gris, this shift of cubism from an analytic to a synthetic art was intimately tied to a redefinition of the function of analysis itself. Gris's analysis of the world became consciously selective. Instead of the painter's choice of subject matter being an arbitrary procedure—a miscellaneous inventory—his choice of subject matter from the world was consciously tied to the ultimate goal of fitting the world into the overall design and unity in his canvas. Near the end of "On the Possibilities of Painting" (1924) he would write:

> The role of aesthetic analysis is to break down the material world, in order to select from it elements of the same category.
> Technique should serve to elaborate all these formal elements into a coherent unity. Its role is synthetic.[25]

Thus when Gris breaks down the things of his world into their parts—the fragmentation and metonymy characteristic of analytic cubist painting—he is doing so in order to reveal the *formal* similarities of these diverse things. In *Violin et Damier* (1913) Gris literally rhymes different elements in the painting. Christopher Gray has described the painting's "rhyme" scheme: it consists "of the almost literal repetition of the same linear theme element in a number of different contexts. . . . Elements derived from the outline of the violin are repeated in the drapery on both the right and the left of the table, while another rhyme, derived from the neck of the violin, is repeated in the pattern of the wall paper in the background and in the outline of the dark shadow just below center on the left margin."[26] Gray also notes that Gris extends the notion of rhyming by establishing metaphoric relationships among the objects, although "the difference between rhymes and metaphors is not always clear." The difference lies in the fact that "a metaphor points out a comparison, rather than a simple rhythmical repetition, as can be seen for example in Gris's *Guitare, Verre et Bouteille* (1914), where there is an obvious comparison of the round aperture of the guitar to the lip of the glasses."[27] Perhaps the distinction between "rhyme" and "metaphor" in Gris's painting can be seen most clearly if we turn to *The Open Window*. There is a distinct rhyme between the aperture of the guitar and the black oval which sits in the bottle's shadow. Another rhyme occurs between the three smaller ovals at the top of the bottle, in its shadow, and to the left in the dark form which appears to be a pipe. The large and small ovals, together with the circular forms of the grapes, stand in metaphoric relation: they suggest one another without duplicating one another. A metaphor exists also between the shape of the guitar and the cloud formation. A metaphoric mirror image can be seen in the wave of the line which connects the bottom of the guitar, the bottle, and the music, and in its inverse in the wave of the hills out the window. The staff lines of the music rhyme with the strings of the guitar, and both find metaphors in the lines that cross and pattern the sea and in the shape of the shutter slats.

The "rhyme" of Gris's painting is the technical device which establishes patterns of repetition within the painting. And Gris's "metaphor," like Williams's in the "Primrose," defines the relations that exist between the diverse objects of the world. Suzanne Juhasz has pointed out in her study of *Metaphor and the Poetry of Williams, Pound, and Stevens* that Williams's "use of metaphor is fundamental to the structure of his poetry" because it both suggests "the essentially divorced condition of modern life" and brings the things in this divorced and multiplicitous world "together as closely as possible for the purpose of revelation" of formal "unity."[28] Gris's painterly metaphor suggests the same revelation of a formal unity which transcends the divorced condition of the world. Furthermore, it is clear that Gris's work is the product of the same dialectic between mind and matter that we find in Williams. Gris defines the modern experience of form as the expression of a concrete reality which belongs to the human mind alone, in which the mind represents itself and which is finally the "coherent unity" or abstract design of the canvas. The objective world remains for Gris a vast disarray of things which he must analyze in order to detect the "elements of the same category" which will allow him to realize this purely formal unity.

Shortly after Williams read Gris's "Possibilities of Painting" in the *transatlantic review,* he acknowledged his debt to cubist painting in general in the poem "This Florida: 1924" (*CEP,* 329–31). Since Gris was at this time Williams's favorite painter, we can safely assume that when he acknowledges his debt to cubism he is acknowledging Gris in particular. The poem is about Williams's effort to escape the barrenness of winter which had occupied him so thoroughly in the *Sour Grapes* years. He has joined the "frantic pilgrimage" to the South, "Florida the Flowery," in order to "escape"

> this winter
> this winter that I feel.

His expectation, and ours, is that he will discover an abstract design for the poem in this flowering environment. But if he has escaped winter, he has not escaped the winter that he feels, a winter of the soul sustained by his inability to discover any adequate pattern. He tries three separate designs, and they all fail. First he considers the possibility of a traditional pattern:

> Shall I write it in iambs?
> Cottages in a row
>
> all radioed and showerbathed?
> But I am sick of rime—
> The whole damned town
>
> is riming up one street
> and down another

Traditional rhyme and metric organization are rejected by force of the pun he makes on "rime" which is equally frost, the stuff of winter. There is, however, a different kind of "rime," the rime discovered in dada's "senseless/ unarrangment of wild things":

> there is
> the rime of her white teeth
> the rime of glasses
> at my plate, the ripple time
> the rime her fingers make

The pun at work in his consideration of traditional patterns of organization is still in force here. By this "unarrangement," he notes, "we thought to escape rime" (traditional patterns, and by extension winter), but this he realizes to be "the stupidest rime of all," for it embraces chaos and disorder in a way that would deny the flowering of the poem. Finally, and as we have come to expect of him, he would "rather" organize the poem in a way that is parallel to "those varying shades/ of orange" which comprise an hibiscus blossom and which are

> the shades and textures
> of a Cubist picture
>
> the charm
> of fish by Hartley, orange
> of ale and lilies
>
> orange of topaz, orange of red hair
> orange of curaçao
> orange of the Tiber
>
> turbid, orange of the bottom
> rocks in Maine rivers
> orange of mushrooms

of Cepes that Marshal loved
to cook in copper
pans, orange of the sun—

Here we have an "unarrangement" of many things unified by
the overriding image of the hibiscus blossom, the repetition of
the three-line stanza and the repetition of the word "orange" in
a manner that is meant to call to mind the repetition of forms
and colors in cubist work. But Williams seems to turn away
from this effort to unify the multiplicity of his world by turning
to, of all things, urine samples:

I shall do my pees, instead—
boiling them in test tubes
holding them to the light

dropping in the acid—
Peggy has a little albumen
in hers—

The synthesizing powers of the imagination seem to be replaced
here by scientific and analytic reasoning. At the same time we
have turned from a consideration of exotic, beautiful, and in-
herently artistic material to a consideration of the mundane, the
base, and the inartistic. Williams's diction has changed from an
elevated and complex syntax and vocabulary to the simple and
direct address of colloquial speech and usage, discovered in the
formal composition of paintings such as Gris's.

He now records a movement back to an analysis of the inartistic ground of winter where art has not as yet been achieved,
a world of urine as opposed to hibiscus. In this sense, the last
stanzas underscore Williams's continuing inability to discover a
satisfactory formal arrangement capable of sustaining his vision.
But there seems to me at least as much contact as divorce between the last urine-sample stanzas and the abstract pattern
achieved in his earlier presentation of the orange "shades and
textures" of Florida. The catalogue of shades and textures ends
by noting the "orange of the sun," and his pattern of color—
mirrored in the contraction of the poem's stanzaic patterns —
extends to his return to the mundane, his yellow "pees" held up
against "the light." What Williams is positing here is that ab-

straction and composition can be extended to include in their design even the most direct treatment of the coarsest "thing." As he says early in *A Novelette* (the book which champions Gris's "conversation as design"), "Learn to write and to make a smooth page no matter what the incoherence of the day . . . to keep ordered the disorder of the pageless actual" (*I*, 274–75). Or as Juan Gris puts it in "The Possibilities of Painting": "It is a question at fitting this rather shapeless world into . . . formal necessities."[29]

For Williams, composition—that is, the formal design and structure of the poem—becomes a way to sustain his formless subject matter. In this sense, Williams's "Dish of Fruit" (*CEP*, 91) is written in the spirit of Gris's *Dish of Pears*. The poem reads, in its entirety:

> The table describes
> nothing: four legs, by which
> it becomes a table. Four lines
> by which it becomes a quatrain,
>
> the poem that lifts the dish
> of fruit, if we say it is like
> a table—how will it describe
> the contents of the poem?

Both the *table* and the *poem*, similar designs composed of four legs/lines and each lifting a dish of fruit, one literally and the other titularly, *as forms* describe nothing: forms are, in themselves, "sense"-less. Design has nothing whatever to do with subject matter, with the dish of fruit. But the quatrain, a purely formal and abstract design, is *"like/ a table,"* and in this way Williams brings the abstract design which is the poem to a representational and particular subject matter. Like the table, the quatrains support the poem's subject matter, the dish of fruit. As the poem's metaphor suggests, the poem is about two things: the literal dish of fruit on the table, and *writing about* the literal dish of fruit on the table, the imagination which must confront the dish of fruit. The poem is to the table as the writing or the imagination is to the world, as abstraction is to reality. The point Williams is making is that abstract form does not in fact describe or define the world because it works independently of the world. But what abstract form does accomplish is a *composition* of the world. It elevates the world to a point where we can appreciate it aesthetically, as both table and poem elevate the dish of fruit. Conversely, in bringing an abstract form to a subject matter—the quatrain to the table—the imagination makes contact with the world and is rescued from the "altitude" where the world is left behind. The poem is a conversation between mind and matter, and its "fruit" lies in the fact that the conversation can take place at all. For Williams, the conversation between the concrete and the abstract represents, in fact, "the cure" which is discovered when we come "to the secret of that form/ interknit with the unfathomable ground/ where we walk daily" ("The Cure," *CLP*, 23), a sentiment which echoes Juan Gris's belief that "painting . . . is like a fabric, all of a piece and uniform, with one set of threads as the representational . . . and the cross-threads as the . . . abstract."[30] From the realization of this conversation the tapestry which is *Paterson* would finally be woven.

NOTES

1. The letter to Williams is reprinted in full in *A Return to Pagany: The History, Correspondence, and Selections from a Little Magazine 1929–1932*, ed. Stephen Halpert with Richard Johns (Boston: Beacon Press, 1969), p. 3.

2. William Carlos Williams, "Manifesto," *Pagany* 1 (January-March, 1930): 1.

3. T. S. Eliot, "Charleston, Hey! Hey!" *The Nation and Athenaeum* 40 (January 29, 1927): 525.

4. Quoted in John Malcolm Brinnin, *The Third Rose: Gertrude Stein and Her World* (Boston: Little, Brown, 1959), p. 239.

5. Yvor Winters, *In Defense of Reason: A Study of American Experimental Poetry* (Chicago: Swallow Press, n.d.), pp. 83, 86. Edmund Wilson dedicates a chapter to Stein's work and includes Tristan Tzara's "Memoirs of Dadaism" as an appendix in *Axel's Castle: A Study in the Imaginative Literature of 1870–1930* (1931; reprint, New York: Scribner's, 1958), pp. 237–56, 304–12. Perhaps Winters caused Williams to temper his *Pagany* "Manifesto" and his essay on Stein. In the letter to Johns in which Williams agreed to write the manifesto (July 12, 1929), Williams writes: "And what will Ivor Winter's [*sic*] say? He

is already ill over my lack of godliness or ecclesiasticil [*sic*] organization or evil nature or general cussedness" (*A Return to Pagany*, p. 12).

6. William Carlos Williams, "Further Announcements," *Contact* 1 (December 20, 1920): 10. The most complete summary of Williams's always ambiguous relation to dada can be found in Dickran Tashjian's *Skyscraper Primitives*. But while Tashjian contrasts the "deliberately incoherent phenomenon" of dada to the more programmatic movements of the time like cubism and surrealism (see especially p. 13), it is clear that Williams (and many of his contemporaries) saw dada as merely the most radical expression of a general spirit that could be detected at work, to a greater or lesser degree, in all modern art.

7. Richard Huelsenbeck, *En Avant Dada: A History of Dadaism*, trans. Ralph Manheim, reprinted in *The Dada Painters and Poets*, ed. Robert Motherwell, *The Documents of Modern Art*, Vol. 8 (New York: Wittenborn, 1967), pp. 42, 37 (my emphasis). In *Skyscraper Primitives* Tashjian is careful to emphasize the affirmative and creative drift of dada—its "negation redounded to affirmation; its destructive sweep released the individual from moribund restrictions to explore new realms of expression" (pp. 11–12)—and, like me, he emphasizes Williams's interest in dada's creative side.

8. Roman Jakobson, "Poetry of Grammar and Grammar of Poetry," in *Selected Writings*, III (The Hague: Mouton, 1981), pp. 94, 87.

9. Dikjstra, *Hieroglyphics*, p. 165; Miller, *Poets of Reality*, pp. 306–7.

10. "Why he selected Some Flower Studies," in *This Is My Best: Over 150 Self-Chosen and Complete Masterpieces, Together with Their Reasons for Their Selection*, ed. Whit Burnett (New York: Dial, 1942), p. 641.

11. One of "Two Poems," *Manuscripts* 1 (February 1922): 15.

12. Introduction to Charles Henri Ford's *The Garden of Disorder and Other Poems* (London: Europa Press, 1938), p. 9.

13. I have made use here of three very comprehensive and useful summaries of surrealist style: Mary Ann Caws, *The Poetry of Dada and Surrealism: Aragon, Breton, Tzara, Eluard and Desnos* (Princeton: Princeton University Press, 1970), especially pp. 20–36; the chapter on "The Surrealist Image," pp. 140–69 of Anna Balakian's *Surrealism: The Road to the Absolute* (1959; rev. ed., New York: Dutton, 1970); and Michael Benedikt's superb introduction to *The Poetry of Surrealism: An Anthology* (Boston: Little, Brown, 1974).

14. "Midas: A Proposal for a Magazine," *SE*, 244. Williams's interest in beginning *Midas*, with André Breton's protege Nicolas Calas, led to the subsequent invitation to co-edit *VVV* with Breton. Two useful surveys of Williams's ties to the surrealists in the 1940s are the chapters "Fantastic America," in Mike Weaver's *William Carlos Williams: The American Background* (Cambridge: Cambridge University

Press, 1971), pp. 128–56, and Tashjian's treatment in the chapter "Proletarian Portraits" of *William Carlos Williams and the American Scene,* especially pp. 132–36.

15. Wassily Kandinsky, *Concerning the Spiritual in Art,* trans. Michael Sadleir et al., *The Documents of Modern Art,* Vol. 5 (New York: Wittenborn, 1947), p. 77.

16. Letter dated 25 March 1921, *Letters of Juan Gris,* trans. and ed. Douglas Cooper (London: privately printed, 1956), p. 105.

17. Gris, "Possibilities," pp. 199–200.

18. Gris, 1921 Statement for *L'Esprit Nouveau,* reprinted in Kahnweiler, *Juan Gris,* p. 193.

19. I mean here to begin to disassociate Williams's work from any organicist theory of form. While he did, early in his career, discover form rising from his material (in, for instance, the famous title poem of *Spring and All,* where "One by one objects are defined—/ It quickens: clarity, outline of leave" [*CEP,* 241]), he more and more avoided the synthetic vision of form and content which an organic theory implies until, in his late work, he shunned it almost altogether. In this I stand against most approaches to the formal dimension of Williams's work. I have more to say on this point later.

20. Haftmann, *Painting in the Twentieth Century,* I, 203.

21. In order to make my own argument clearer, I have taken the liberty of consolidating and abridging several paragraphs of Williams's rather diffuse text here. Williams probably derived the phrase "conversation as design" from Gris's "Des Possibilités de la Peinture" which appeared in French in two parts in the *transatlantic review* 1, no. 6 (1924): 482–86 and 2, no. 1 (1924): 75–79. "Conversation" is a reasonable translation for Gris's concluding statement that "la seule possibilité de la peinture est l'expression de certains *rapports* du peinture avec le monde extérieur" and that the painting itself "est l'association intime de ces *rapports* entre eux." And "design" is a reasonable equivalent for the "architecture des elements formels" which, for Gris, reveals this "association intime."

22. This discussion is part of Williams's prose discussion of Gris's work that is interrupted by the poems "The Rose" and "At the Faucet of June." Before the poems are introduced, Williams writes that there is a picture of Juan Gris, which he has never seen in color, that defines "what the modern trend is." In *The Hieroglyphics of a New Speech* (p. 174), Bram Dijkstra, apparently ignoring Williams's continuing discussion after the poems, has asserted that the picture to which Williams refers is Gris's 1914 collage *Roses,* and that the poem "The Rose" is an attempt to realize this painting in poetic language. However, I can discover no reproduction, black and white or otherwise, of *Roses* in any publication before 1930. *The Open Window,* on the other hand, was reproduced in *Broom* 1 (January 1922): p. 264, and in

black and white. Most of Dijkstra's other examples of Williams's poetic realizations of specific plastic works are similarly suspect. I have discussed this issue a little more fully in my "Distancing 'The Rose' from *Roses*," *William Carlos Williams Newsletter* 5 (Spring 1979): 18–19, where I do note that both "The Rose" and *Roses* quite possibly share a common reference to the work of Gertrude Stein.

23. Letter dated 26 March 1915, *Letters*, p. 26.

24. Reprinted in Kahnweiler, *Juan Gris*, p. 193.

25. Ibid., p. 201.

26. Christopher Gray, *Cubist Aesthetic Theories* (Baltimore: Johns Hopkins University Press, 1953), p. 98.

27. Ibid., pp. 98–99. It is on the authority of D.-H. Kahnweiler, Gris's lifelong friend, biographer and dealer, that Gray labels these formal devices "rhyme" and "metaphor." Kahnweiler says that Gris thought of them as such in *Juan Gris*, pp. 140–41.

28. Suzanne Juhasz, *Metaphor and the Poetry of Williams, Pound, and Stevens* (Lewisburg, Penn.: Bucknell University Press, 1974), pp. 13–14.

29. Gris, "Possibilities," p. 220.

30. Ibid.

CHAPTER TWO

Shaping America

Williams had defined the object of his poetic effort, almost from the outset, to be the discovery of poetic form equal to the task of embodying the multiplicity of the American scene. In a 1917 article entitled "America, Whitman, and the Art of Poetry," he was willing to admit that Whitman's enumeration of the array of American objects was the "rock" upon which American poetry was founded, and that Whitman's greatest achievement was that in this enumeration he had "destroyed the forms antiquity decreed him to take and use." Whitman's legacy, however, lay in the necessity for American poets to make "a new verse form" of his unruly democracy vistas:

> American verse of today must have a certain quality of freedom, must be "free verse" in a sense. It must be new verse, in a new conscious form. But even more than that it must be free in that it is free to include all temperaments, all phases of our environment, physical as well as spiritual, mental and moral. It must be truly democratic, truly free for all—and yet it must be governed.
>
> This is no small demand to make a new verse form. Its elements must not be too firmly cemented together as they are in the aristocratic forms of past civilizations. They must be perfectly concrete or they will escape through the fingers—but they must not be rigidly united. . . . The elements of the new form must be simple and single so that they are capable of every form of moulding.[1]

This essay anticipates by several years Williams's familiarity with the paintings of Juan Gris, but it already champions the simplicity of form which he would later come to admire in Gris's work. More important, it sees in that simplicity of form a way to overcome an art which consists of little more than an "inventory of objects."

According to Williams's later testimony in the *Autobiography*, his emphasis upon finding this new verse form separated his poetry early on from its imagist roots. For a time he had followed Pound's imagist rules, the famous "Dont's," but he had done so "merely to fill out a standard form" (*A*, 148). And even the standard poetical forms of imagism "ran quickly out": imagism, "though it had been useful in ridding the field of verbiage, had no formal necessity implicit in it. It had already dribbled off into so called 'free verse' which, as we saw, was a misnomer. There is no such thing as free verse! Verse is measure of some sort. 'Free verse' was without measure and needed none for its projected objectifications. Thus the poem had run down and become formally non extant" (*A*, 264).

Williams saw himself as moving quickly beyond the influence of both Whitman and Pound because, unlike them, he emphasized what he later called "the structural approach" to poetry. "The *structural approach* has two phases," he told an audience in Puerto Rico on April 19, 1941, "the first, the selection of forms from poems already achieved, to restuff them with metaphysical and other matter, and, the second, to parallel the inventive impetus of other times with structural concepts derived from our own day. . . . The first is *weak* and the second is *strong*."[2] Whitman and the imagists, Williams believed, had either no structural dimension at all or, at best, a weak one. Williams insisted that his own verse possess itself of the strong. In the revelation of "structural concepts derived from our own day," modern painting would be his most important model.

Pound, too, in developing his imagist maxims, had turned to the example of the plastic arts. His most articulate defense of imagism occurs in his memoir of the French sculptor Gaudier-Brzeska. But where Pound's concern with Brzeska leads him to write that "the image is the poet's pigment," and that "it is our affair to render the *image* as we have perceived or conceived it,"[3] Williams responds to Brzeska in his 1915 "Vortex" by writing that "in the geometric sense" he would use "words instead of stone" to forge an art of his own (*RI*, 57–58). Pound's concern is one of subject matter, Williams's one of structure and form. The imagist poem, as Pound defined it, recorded that "instant when a thing outward and objective transforms itself . . . into a thing inward and subjective." Thus his outward "faces in the crowd" are visualized imaginatively as "petals on a wet, black bough."[4] Though Williams's "Wheelbarrow" bows in the direction of the mind in its opening stanza—"so much depends/ upon"—it never gives us the *kind* of verbal image that the second, "petals" line of Pound's "Station" gives us. It would seem, in fact, that Williams willfully refuses to visualize the mind in verbal terms; instead, he seems to concentrate almost exclusively on verbalizing material reality.

This refusal has generated a good deal of confusion about and misreading of not only "The Red Wheelbarrow" but also Williams's entire poetic achievement. It has caused J. Hillis Miller to speak of Williams giving up the "ego" in order to "leap into things." Even more typically, James Guimond asserts that "The Red Wheelbarrow" marks the beginning of a "Radical Imagism" which is "characterized by its extremely stark presentation of commonplace objects" to the exclusion of "inner realities." Robert Bly concludes that Williams deals "with outward things— but no inward life."[5] All three have fallen victim to a general trend in art-historical discussions of American modernism which see the Americans artists' interests in objective reality as a "dilution" of the formal necessities they had inherited from European modernism. Abraham A. Davidson, for instance, argues that such American painters as John Marin, Charles Demuth, and Charles Sheeler were "unable to reconcile themselves to or even understand the ambiguities which were at the heart of European Cubism. . . . What emerges . . . is an uncertain melange of Cubist passages which are never completely digested or integrated . . . a style marked by severe simplifications."[6] To the contrary, the Americans' return to the object can be read more productively as the extension, rather than the dilution, of European formal exploration.

None of the American artists with whom Williams associated—not even the photographers—considered their admittedly "stark presentation of commonplace objects" to be an end in itself. "Anything that the poet can effectively lift from its dull bed by force of imagination becomes his material. Anything," Williams wrote. "The commonplace, the tawdry, the sordid all have their poetic uses if the imagination can lighten them."[7] The same could be said of the American artist generally, but the point is that the imagination must work upon the object if the object is to be of use. Art uses "the banal to escape the banal," as Williams put it in 1939 (*SE*, 236), and it escapes the banal by discovering form. The photographer Paul Strand saw in the vitalization of both photography and architecture by the American modern an expression of *"the very necessity of evolving a new form."*[8] Alfred Stieglitz, the photographer who can be considered mentor to this entire generation of American artists, claimed that the inspiration for his pivotal 1907 photograph *The Steerage* lay in the fact that he "saw shapes related to one another—a picture of shapes."[9] In reviewing an exhibition of Greek art for *The Arts* in 1925, Charles Sheeler described a similar interest in the formal foundation of the "objectively" presented object: "The geometric basis of Greek art was the internal structure, skillfully concealed, around which was built the objective aspect of nature with all its sensorial attributes."[10] And he would say later of his 1929 painting *Upper Deck:* "This is what I had been getting ready for. I had come to feel that a picture could have incorporated in it the structural design implied in abstraction and be presented in a wholly realistic manner."[11]

There is probably no better or more concise definition of the American extension of European formal exploration than Sheeler's. Sheeler ties the abstract to the particular, reveals the abstract in the particular. Whenever Williams writes about the painters of the Stieglitz circle, he emphasizes this synthetic vision of the abstract in the concrete. In his introduction to the catalogue of Sheeler's retrospective exhibition at the Museum of Modern Art, *Paintings-Drawings-Photographs, 1939*, Williams writes that it is in "the abstract if you will but left by the artist integral with its native detail . . . in the shape of the thing" that the artist's power lies (*SE*, 233). Significantly, Williams adds that

Alfred Stieglitz. *The Steerage*. 1907. Photogravure (artist's proof) from *Camera Work*, No. 36, 1911, size of print 7¾ x 6½". Collection The Museum of Modern Art, New York. Gift of Alfred Stieglitz.

Charles Sheeler. *Upper Deck*. 1929. Oil on canvas, 74 x 56.3 cm. Courtesy of the Fogg Art Museum, Harvard University. Purchase—Louise E. Bettens Fund.

the "abstract" must make contact with detail because artistic composition is only achieved "in things . . . not beyond them." In his celebration of the "cool and thorough organizations today about us, familiar in industry," in his formal composition of the industrial landscape, Sheeler restores to us the power "to see" (*SE*, 234). As Williams would write in a 1944 poem, when the mind allows itself to consider "The World Narrowed to a Point" (*CLP*, 20), when "the eye awakes," we "focus the wit/ on a world of form."

In "This Florida" Williams had posited that the idea of abstract design was capable of composing the most varied sorts of things. In "The Crimson Cyclamen" (*CEP*, 397–404), his memorial poem to Charles Demuth written shortly after Demuth's death in 1935, Williams emphasizes the imaginative strength of a mind such as Demuth's, capable of composing a flower which is "day by day changing" and which moves constantly toward the "formless":

> Upon each leaf it is
> a pattern more
> of logic than a purpose
> links each part to the rest,
> an abstraction
> playfully following
> centripetal
> devices, as of pure thought—
> . . . .
>
> Such are the leaves
> freakish, of the air
> as thought is.

The poem is full of purposeful ambiguities and puns which simultaneously enforce the multiplicity of its meanings and bring that multiplicity back toward a vision of unity. The petals are "all acolor" (rose, crimson, blue, yellow), but equally, like his oranges in "This Florida," all *a* color ("yet the effect . . . is crimson"). The petals "flare . . . ec*centri*cally" and "formless," and yet they are designed into one "centri*petal*." Finally, the force of the "petal tips/ merging into one flower" is "color only and a form."

The aesthetic thinking behind the integration of abstract design and myriad realistic details in the paintings of men like Demuth was based on the example of Alfred Stieglitz's photography. Members of the Stieglitz circle generally agreed with the distinction Marius de Zayas made between "Photography and Artistic Photography" in a summer 1913 number of *Camera Work:*

> The difference between Photography and Artistic-Photography is that, in the former, man tries [by photographing forms which exist in objective reality] to get at that objectivity of Form, which generates the different conceptions that man has of Form, while the second uses the objectivity of Form [that is, form as it exists in reality] to express a preconceived idea in order to convey an emotion. . . . In the first, man tries to represent something that is outside himself; in the second he tries to represent something in himself. The first is free and impersonal research, while the second is a systematic and personal representation.[12]

The distinction is useful because it equates the "artistic" with the expressive; that is, in art, form originates in the self, not in the world. De Zayas posits that in the kind of scientific analysis that marked early cubism, for instance, one discovers form *in the world,* but in true art one imposes a preconceived idea of form upon the world and verifies the form's authenticity by bringing it back to reality, by insisting that form and reality make contact.

In the final number of *Camera Work* in 1917 de Zayas's notion of artistic photography was made wholly articulate. In that issue Paul Strand, a young photographer whom Stieglitz had recently taken into the circle, published a series of photographs a number of which, as Strand himself explained, presented "objects . . . used as abstract forms, to create an emotion unrelated to the objectivity as such." These photographs, *Wall Street* and *Abstraction, Porch Shadows* among them, carried on what Stieglitz had begun in *The Steerage.* "It is in the organization of this objectivity," Strand continued, "that the photographer's point of view toward Life enters in, and where formal conception born of the emotions, the intellect, or of both, is as inevitably necessary for him, before an exposure is made, as for

Paul Strand. *Abstraction, Porch Shadows, Twin Lakes, Connecticut, 1915.*
Gelatin-silver print, 13¹⁄₁₆ x 9¹⁄₁₆". Collection The Museum of Modern Art,
New York. Gift of Arthur Bellowa. © 1982 The Paul Strand Foundation.

the painter, before he puts his brush to canvas."[13] As in *The Steerage*, formal design is seen as the representation of the mind and objective detail as the representation of the material world; the photograph integrates the two. Photography, of all the media the most suited to direct treatment of the thing, reveals also the powerful abstracting and ordering capabilities of the mind at work on the various things that make up the world. Furthermore, material reality in its most inartistic manifestations—in the industrial scene which so intrigued Sheeler, in the mundane objectivity of a porch railing, in the materialism and barrenness of *Wall Street* or the chaotic deck of *The Steerage*—is, if the mind makes contact with it, potentially the stuff of art.

Nowhere is this more apparent than in Stieglitz's two major series of photographs executed from the early 1920s into the 1930s, *Songs of the Sky* and *Equivalents*. "The use of clouds," Stieglitz would say, "has made people less aware of clouds as clouds. . . . People seem freer to think about the relationships in the pictures than about the subject matter for its own sake."[14] Earlier he had described Strand's abstract photographs as the "brutally direct . . . expression of today,"[15] and he extended this sentiment—the expression of the facts as they are, not as we would have them—to the *Equivalents*: "My photographs are a picture of the chaos in the world, and of my relationship to that chaos. My prints show the world's constant upsetting of man's equilibrium, and his eternal battle to reestablish it." The equilibrium is reestablished through Stieglitz's recognition that the abstract forms he has discovered in the clouds are "equivalent" to the workings of his own mind, in much the same way that a completely abstract painting can be taken as the objective manifestation of a subjective stance: "it is only after I have created an equivalent of what has moved me that I can begin to think about its significance. Shapes, as such, do not interest me unless they happen to be an outer equivalent of something already taking form within me."[16]

II

For Stieglitz the function of art is to "reestablish equilibrium" in a chaotic world by imposing "shape" upon a recalcitrant reality. This is, of course, a straightforward humanistic position and one which he shares with most of the writers and artists of his time, especially the New Critics. And like the New Critics, Stieglitz invests his project with formal organicism. This is what he means by the word "equilibrium"—that is, he wishes to establish a harmony between form and content, and if at first his form is wholly subjective it must be transformed in the photograph so that it appears to have arisen inevitably from the photograph's objective subject matter. In this way mind and matter are synthesized, the world is composed. The world justifies the artist's imagination—and his imagination forms the world.

For a long time Williams embraced notions more or less consonant with these. The prose in *Spring and All* is full of comparable ideas. Indeed, it is possible to argue that Williams never quite gave up an organicist theory of art—at least not when he was trying to explain or defend his work to others. As I shall argue later, his notoriously inadequate explanations of the so-called variable foot are most usefully seen as efforts to defend as organic what through the 1940s and 1950s is more and more evidently a formally mechanical and arbitrary practice. (I do not mean to demean this mechanical theory of artistic form—I merely adopt Schlegel's classic distinction.) I think it is fair to say that the times were so thoroughly prejudiced in favor of an organic theory that Williams tended to believe he had to have one himself, even when he had apparently forsaken it.

Williams's humanism is another matter, though it is considerably different from a New Critical variety by virtue of his insistence that form and content need not harmonize or achieve equilibrium so much as they ought merely to cooperate antagonistically, as he would have it by the time he wrote the fourth book of *Paterson* in the early 1950s. In fact, the necessity of art's imposition of order—albeit a wholly inorganic and arbitrary order—upon the world is a notion from which Williams would never retreat. Where he differs from his contemporaries is in his willingness to let the world stand as it is, in his sense that if art were really to succeed in its humanist project, if it were in fact able to *compose* the world, then art would annihilate itself. Williams's art needs a world outside itself—and a world outside, moreover, finally resistant to its formal impositions.

For Williams, whose poetry seems to be based completely upon a collision of values—art and reality, design and detail, the multiplicitous and the single—the city would seem the ideal image. "From cubism and futurism, Duchamp and Schwitters, to the present," art critic William Seitz writes, "the proper backdrop . . . [for modern art] has been the multifarious fabric of the modern city—its random patchwork of slickness and deterioration, cold planning and liberating confusion, resplendent beauty and noxious squalor. The cityscape gives striking evidence of the world-wide collision of moralities and panaceas, facts and propagandas, and sets in relief the countless images— tender, comic, tragic, or drably neutral—of contemporary life."[17] But the city is a source of confusion in Williams's art and in the art of American modernism as a whole. The same competing aesthetic visions which confront Williams whenever he looks at the cityscape dominate his poetry through the 1930s and 1940s: does he accept the city for what it is, in all its chaos and its pluralism? Or does he impose the singleness of his artistic vision—that is, order—upon it?

None of Williams's contemporaries approached the city with anything close to a sense of ease, and Williams himself certainly was no exception. Despite the sure knowledge that the city embodied modernity, to write about it or paint it demanded certain aesthetic decisions—very basic ones, such as whether or not to organize the canvas or the page—which the plurality of the city itself denied. In an important and suggestive study Donald B. Kuspit has pointed out that most American artists attempt to come to terms with the dilemmas the city presents by forcing themselves to humanize or naturalize it, thereby "neutralizing its impact and assimilating it to known modes of experience."[18] Stieglitz's famous photograph of the Flatiron Building (1903) reduces the skyscraper to the dimensions of a tree and softens its hard edges with a snowstorm. Similarly, paintings like Georgia O'Keeffe's *The Radiator Building—Night, New York* (1929)

Alfred Stieglitz. *The Flatiron*. 1902–3. Photogravure on vellum from *Camera Work*, No. 4, 1903, size of print 12⅞ x 6⅝″. Collection The Museum of Modern Art, New York. Purchase.

or John Marin's *Lower Manhattan* (1922) transform the city into the image of a flower, both O'Keeffe's building and Marin's street scene assuming the shape of an open blossom. Such images of New York proliferate throughout American modernist painting; and they help us to think that it is we who control the city, and not that the city controls us. But speaking first of Stieglitz's *Flatiron* and then moving on to the rest of American modern art, Kuspit points out that there is

> a lurking malaise about the building. However much we "soften" it atmospherically, or subjectivize it by estheticizing it, we are still not at home with it. It looms in the background as an ominous presence, not at all subsumed by the scene of which it is a part, too unnatural to be an altogether acceptable part of it. A construction epitomizing the modernity of New York—and modernity expresses itself through novel constructions—is naturalized, and so neutralized as modern. We will see that the treating of modern constructions as natural organisms, or as organic parts of nature, becomes a standard way of feeling at home with them— but the very act of doing so implies that modernity is alien. Thus it is experienced from the beginning as a mode of self-estrangement as well as of self-expression.[19]

Kuspit is writing art history, but the applicability of his insight to a modern American literary theory seems to me beyond question—at least as far as Williams's work is concerned. By treating modern constructions—poems as well as Flatiron buildings—as natural organisms, Williams is able, for a while, to feel at home with them. But Williams comes to recognize, sooner than most, the self-estrangement implicit in his project, and this sense of estrangement prompts him to abandon the synthetist dream. The city—New York or Paterson—does not resolve the conflicts it embodies; it simply defines a space in which its conflicting parts compete.

But for Stieglitz—and for the early Williams—the chaos and tension of the city are clearly something to fear, something for art to defeat. Stieglitz's recollections about his feelings toward New York and its skyscrapers are exemplary:

> From 1893 to 1895 I often walked the streets of New York downtown, near the East River, taking my hand camera with me.

John Marin. *Lower Manhattan (Composing Derived from Top of Woolworth).* 1922. Water-color and charcoal with paper cutout attached with thread, 21⅝ x 26⅞". Collection The Museum of Modern Art, New York. Acquired through the Lillie P. Bliss Bequest.

I wandered around the Tombs, the old Post Office, Five Points.
I loathed the dirty streets, yet I was fascinated.

. . . .

In the early months of 1903 I stood spellbound during a great
snow storm before the Flat Iron building. It had just been erected
on 23rd Street at the junction of Fifth Avenue and Broadway.

Watching the structure go up, I felt no desire to photograph
the different stages of its development. But with the trees of
Madison Avenue covered with fresh snow, The Flat Iron im-
pressed me as never before. It appeared to be moving toward me
like the bow of a monster ocean steamer—a picture of new America still in the making.[20]

The language here is fascinating, for the building remains a
monster even as it leaves Stieglitz enraptured. And to see an
ocean steamer which promises the making of a new America is
willfully to see the building (and, by extension, America) with
the immigrant's same trusting naiveté, not only softened by the
snow but purified as well. The wonder of Stieglitz's vision —
and his photograph—is the wonder of metamorphosis, the "dirty
streets" of New York almost magically cleansed.

Until the late 1940s there is about American modernism a
consistent sense of *amelioration* of which Stieglitz's vision of
the Flatiron Building is typical. Marius de Zayas would claim
in *Camera Work* that in his art Stieglitz "worked in the American
spirit. He married Man to Machinery and he obtained issue."[21]
This kind of rhetoric not only characterizes Stieglitz as a kind
of artistic Carnegie, but it makes the American industrialist into
a kind of artist as well (a point not lost on Henry Ford, who
hired Charles Sheeler to immortalize his new River Rouge Plant
in a striking series of thirty-two photographs in 1927). To the
American modernist, art simply makes things better. John Marin,
a painter whom Stieglitz championed very early on and whom
Williams would later call "a flaming expression of the ground
from which we both sprang" (*RI*, 229), would write that in the
city "great forces [are] at work; great movements; the large
buildings and the small buildings; the warring of the great and
the small. . . . While these powers are at work, pushing, pulling,
sideways, downwards, I can hear the sound of their strife. . . .

And so I try to express graphically what the city is doing. Within the frames there must be balance, a controlling of these warring pushing, pulling, forces. This is what I am trying to realize."[22] Just as Stieglitz's art would cleanse New York City's "dirty streets," Marin's would balance and control New York's strife. This same ameliorative stance holds as late as Ralph Steiner's and Willard Van Dyke's famous 1939 documentary film *The City,* and the difficulties it raises are probably nowhere clearer than in this film. Created for a New York World's Fair which took as its theme "The Golden Age of Science," and narrated by Lewis Mumford, *The City* overtly condemns city life and expounds the potential bliss of life in suburbia. "The choice is yours," Mumford says repeatedly, as the film switches back and forth from visions of pastoral harmony to portrayals of urban dissonance. Clearly the intent of the film is to have us choose the suburban life, where there is no "warring," no "pushing, pulling, sideways, downwards." These forces are not so much controlled in the new suburban landscape as they are missing altogether. As the documentary film's leading expert, John Grierson, noted at the time, "There is something wrong about the Steiner-Van Dyke paradise." The filmmakers claim to be "against metropolitan madness . . . its nervousness, its wasted energies, its dangers, its damnation," but, Grierson says, "I do not believe Steiner and Van Dyke believe a word of it any more than I do: and I have the proof of it the moment they shoot these children on the sidewalk, those domestic jalopies on the metropolitan road, the clamour of the industrial scene, or the open sesame of the automat. Like myself, they are metropolitans. Their cameras get an edge on and defeat their theories."[23] In short, art is the product of the clamor of the city; it is generated by tensions, by conflict. To see the film is to experience the dilemma of American modernism. We begin by thinking we would prefer the homogeneous, controlled paradise of suburbia, but as Mumford repeats "The choice is yours," and as shots of the bland pastoral garden apartments are interspersed with shots of the chaos of the city, we realize that what we long to *see,* what is artistically exciting, is the cityscape. Our ideal—the promise of suburban serenity—seems anemic beside it.

In time Williams would choose the city himself. But like O'Keeffe's and Marin's paintings, many of his earlier poems—such as "Perpetuum Mobile: The City," "The Flower," and "A Marriage Ritual"—equate the city to a flower and thereby suburbanize it, ameliorating its more negative qualities. In "Flight to the City" he metamorphoses it into a kind of a fairyland:

> a crown for her head with
> castles upon it, skyscrapers
> filled with nut-chocolates—
>
>   dovetame winds—
>
> stars of tinsel
>
> from the great end of a cornucopia
> of glass.
>   (*CEP*, 224)

Likewise, in juxtapositions very similar to those Stieglitz creates when he naturalizes the Flatiron Building by placing it inside the frame of a tree, Williams allows, in his tellingly titled "A Bastard Peace" (*CEP*, 414), a "concrete disposal tank" to be graced by "a dandelion in bloom—and a white/ butterfly." "View of a Lake" includes not only a "waste of cinders," a "concrete/ service hut," "a wrecked car," and "stalled traffic," but opposite all this "remains a sycamore/ in leaf" (*CEP*, 96–97). In "The Agonized Spires," New York's bridges pierce "left ventricles/ with long sunburnt fingers" (*CEP*, 263), macabre but humanized nonetheless. And in his "Classic Scene" the industrial landscape is metamorphosed into an image of a couple, one active and the other "passive today," sitting together on a chair.

> A power-house
> in the shape of
> a red brick chair
> 90 feet high
>
> on the seat of which
> sit the figures
> of two metal
> stacks—aluminum—
>   (*CEP*, 407)

Again like Stieglitz's relation to the Flatiron Building, the monstrosity of the scene underscores our alienation from it. But Williams's metaphor nevertheless strives to draw us to it, to make it as accessible and as memorable as our grandparents.[24]

Perhaps Williams's most ameliorative—and attractive—image for the city occurs in his 1930 poem "The Flower" (*CEP*, 236–38). This ambitious poem begins by metamorphosing the city into a flower:

> A petal, colorless and without form
> the oblong towers lie
>
> beyond the low hill and northward the great
> bridge stanchions,
>
> small in the distance, have appeared,
> pinkish and incomplete—
>
> It is the city,
> approaching over the river. Nothing
>
> of it is mine, but visibly
> for all that it is petal of a flower—my own.
>
> It is a flower through which the wind
> combs the whitened grass and a black dog
>
> with yellow legs stands eating from a
> garbage barrel. One petal goes eight blocks

The city is a flower, but a flower awaiting the form and color that only the poet can bring to it. We begin to see that form take shape in the couplets here, a formal duality which mirrors the juxtaposition of the "garbage barrel" and the "petal," the "whitened" and the "black." The city is an image that Williams would like to control, to make his "own." But, as he says later in the poem, he has been "tormented" by it and "unable to say anything much to the point" about it.

What makes the difference in this poem is a second metamorphosis in which Williams compares the city/flower to a woman:

> A flower, at its heart (the stamens, pistil,
> etc.) is naked woman, about 38, just

> out of bed, worth looking at both for
> her body and her mind and what she has seen
>
> and done. She it was put me straight
> about the city.

At the heart of the formless city is a naked woman, and in conversation (contact) with her Williams begins to make form of the city. Each "petal" of the city is organized by her presence at its center. The city as woman maintains, furthermore, the sense of conflict and opposition with which Williams approaches the city in the first place. She is, after all, the male poet's opposite. But as woman the city is suddenly accessible; it even projects the creative union of the poet and his subject, mind and matter.

As early as 1917 Williams had argued, in a long letter to *The Egoist* entitled "The Great Sex Spiral," that male psychology is "characterized by an inability to concede reality to fact . . . the universal lack of attachment between the male and the objective world." Conversely, female psychology moves "toward the earth, toward concreteness":

> Thus man's only positive connexion with the earth is in the fleeting sex function. When not in pursuit of the female man has absolutely no necessity to exist. But this chase can never lead to satisfaction in the catch, never to objective satisfaction, since as soon as the catch is made the objective is removed and nothing remains but to make another catch of the same kind. . . . Thus the male pursuit leads only to further pursuit, that is, not toward the earth, but away from it—not to concreteness, but to further hunting, to star-gazing, to idleness.
>
> . . . . .
>
> [The female] pursuit of the male results not in further chase, at least not in the immediate necessity for further chase, but to definite physical results that connect her indisputably and firmly with the earth at her feet by an unalterable chain, every link of which is concrete. Woman is physically essential to the maintenance of a physical life. . . . To the female mind male psychology (philosophy), which is agnostic, due to his experience, has no reality in her experience. To the female mind such a psychology (philosophy) will always remain a meaningless symbol—a negative attracting her attack.[25]

The opposition and conflict between male and female which
Williams sets out here is equally an opposition between mind
and matter, between the abstracting imagination and the concrete fact. It represents a kind of thinking common to the Stieglitz circle. In 1915 de Zayas had written a poem called "Femme!"
in which the female possesses "pas d'intellectualisme," "pas de
forme," and is "pas le miroir de son male." She is instead "ma-
térialité pure." By implication man is her opposite: "cérébrale"
and "intellectual," he possesses "forme" and is "spiritualité pure."[26]
Similarly, Stieglitz himself responded to a request to write on
the subject "Woman in Art" by saying, "Woman *feels* the World
differently than Man feels it. . . . Man and Woman are *One*
together—potentially One always. The Woman receives the World
through her Womb. That is the seat of her deepest feeling. Mind
comes second."[27] These are essentially the same distinctions that
Williams was still making thirty years later when, in the essay
"Woman as Operator," he argued that a modern painter can
represent the female because she "stands on her feet," whereas
a male cannot be painted because there is only his mind to
represent—and "you might as well try to paint the speed of a
hurricane or the stillness of a desert" (*RI*, 181).[28] The male is
mind; the female is fact. The two make contact only in "the
fleeting sex function"; otherwise they exist in perpetual opposition. Form and content are at odds.

III

The ameliorative bent of Williams's humanism, the shaping
of America which he defines as his project, is tempered by his
sense that synthetic union is fleeting and that opposition and
conflict are the driving forces not only of the world but of his
poetry as well. Any theory of metaphor, for instance, which
would synthesize the original juxtaposition of its terms—that is,
arrive at what Coleridge called the "spirit of unity that blends
and (as it were) fuses each into each"—denies the life of the
poem, urges upon it a formal stasis which Williams would come
to view as the end of art. To return to an earlier example—"My
luv/ is like/ a/ greenglass insulator"—the poem is merely ludi-

crous if metaphor must fuse its terms into some "spirit of unity."
But if metaphor is considered as a formal juxtaposition of terms
which "push and pull" at one another, then the poem becomes,
to borrow the title of one of Williams's longer poems about the
city, "Perpetuum Mobile," a perpetual motion machine, a dynamic "field of action." In this sense Williams is indeed a "poet
of reality," as J. Hillis Miller calls him, not because he leaps into
things, but because he does not deny them. An organic theory
of art, simply put, is a transcendent theory of art. In its drive
toward synthetic unity it seeks to transcend the conflicts of the
world. Williams cannot bring himself to leave the world behind.

But if the chaotic world is necessary to art, so is the shaping
intellect. The shaping capability of imaginative vision is the
point of a poem like "The Great Figure," which would inspire
Demuth's 1928 "poster-portrait" of Williams, *I Saw the Figure
5 in Gold*. There are autobiographical reasons why Demuth
should have chosen to represent this poem—Williams wrote it
on a visit to Demuth and Marsden Hartley—but there are aesthetic reasons as well. What focuses the poem, and later Demuth's painting, is "the figure 5." It organizes the chaotic world
around itself:

> Among the rain
> and lights
> I saw the figure 5
> in gold
> on a red
> firetruck
> moving
> tense
> unheeded
> to gong clangs
> siren howls
> and wheels rumbling
> through the dark city.
>
> (*CEP*, 230)

The urban landscape of the poem is blurred in the refracted light
of a night rain, deafened by the cacophony of clangs and howls,
and made to seem altogether unstable and tumultous by its

central image of tension, speed, and change, which Williams emphasizes both by placing the lines "moving/ tense" at the poem's heart and by moving us in short, tension-ridden, one-word lines through that center. Juxtaposed to this world is the figure 5. The clarity of its vision opposes itself to an almost completely confusing (and, in the context of a fire, destructive) moment, even as the brightness of its gold color on a red field opposes itself to the "dark city." The numerical figure, as Demuth's painting makes clear and Jasper Johns's later reworking of it in *The Black Figure 5* (1960) makes even clearer, is simply an abstraction, a design.[29] If the figure is "unheeded," that is because it has so little to do with the world from which it has been lifted.

Even though artists are supposed to be perceptive enough that they can regularly discover such figures in the world, "The Great Figure" does not possess the kind of formal imperative upon which consistent poetics might be based. Its moment is too contingent. The same can be said of a poem like "The Red Wheelbarrow." Written some four years after "The Great Figure," it nevertheless represents a considerable advance over the earlier poem. At least in "The Red Wheelbarrow" there seems to be a consistent formal pattern operating from stanza to stanza, one which could be repeated in other stanzas in other poems. As Hugh Kenner has pointed out, when read as a simple statement of fact—"so much depends upon a red wheelbarrow glazed with rainwater beside the white chickens"—anybody could justifiably call the poem trivial in the extreme.[30] But as a poem—four recognizably similar stanzas on a page—the scope of this trivial statement of fact is enlarged. So much depends upon the *form* into which Williams molds his material, not the material itself. In *Spring and All,* immediately following the poem Williams makes the distinction between "The Red Wheelbarrow" as prose statement and "The Red Wheelbarrow" as poem clear. "The curriculum of knowledge," he writes, "cannot but be divided into the sciences, the thousand and one groups of data—scientific, philosophic, or whatnot. . . . These things exist, but in a different condition when energized by the imagination. . . . If prose is not accurately adjusted to the exposition of the facts it does not exist. . . . Poetry is something quite different. Poetry has to do with the crystallization of the imagination—the perfection of new forms" (*I*, 138, 140). "The Red Wheelbarrow" in fact defines its own aesthetic significance in our experience of it as one of these new forms.

From this point of view, the material which composes Williams's poem, material chosen from Williams's position as artist, begins to take on the aura of Marcel Duchamp's famous ready-mades. Duchamp had written that the aesthetic dimension of his urinal, *Fountain,* which he had purchased in a plumbing store and submitted to the 1917 New York Independents Exhibition, rested in the fact that he had taken "an ordinary article of life, placed it so that its useful significance disappeared under the new title and point of view—created a new thought for that object."[31] Just as Duchamp revitalizes our aesthetic sense by placing a urinal in the context of art, Williams places his material in an equally strange environment—the poem—and the wheelbarrow's accidental but very material presence in this new context invests it with a new dignity. It is crucial that Williams's material is banal, trivial: by placing this material in the poem, Williams underscores the distance the material has traveled, and the poem defines a radical split between the world of art and the world of barnyards, between a world which crystallizes the imagination and a world which is a mere exposition of the facts.

But both "The Red Wheelbarrow" and the urinal represent the kind of gesture that is largely unrepeatable. As Duchamp surely knew, and as so many younger American artists have sadly discovered, the power which the ready-made possesses lies as much in the uniqueness of its gesture as in anything else. Williams found himself able to repeat the stanzaic form of "The Red Wheelbarrow" only on occasion, most notably in the 1938 poem "Between Walls" (*CEP,* 343) and the 1934 "Proletarian Portrait" (*CEP,* 101). "Between Walls" is overtly about the rise of form out of the trivial and barren world of the city. It describes a broken bottle which lies among an alley's ashes, but which in the context of the poem becomes a new image of the phoenix.[32] "Proletarian Portrait" is a straightforward description of a young woman:

A big young bareheaded woman
in an apron

Her hair slicked back standing
on the street

One stockinged foot toeing
the sidewalk

Her shoe in her hand. Looking
intently into it

She pulls out the paper insole
to find the nail

That has been hurting her

Although the poem is formally indebted to the "Wheelbarrow" stanza, quite clearly Williams has lengthened the "Wheelbarrow" line. Furthermore, he has left the last stanza of "Proletarian Portrait" in a state of incompletion. The changes he has brought about here indicate both the limitations of the "Wheelbarrow" form and the direction in which Williams's poetry would, in time, formally move. When the poem first appeared in a 1934 anthology called *Galaxy,* it was titled "Study for a Figure Representing Modern Culture."[33] By the time it reappeared the following year, both in a magazine and in *An Early Martyr,* Williams had retitled it "Proletarian Portrait." The word "Figure" in the original should be taken, I think, to refer not only to the young woman whom the poem describes, but also to the figure the poem makes, its form. As a study for a form that will represent modern culture, the poem, in lengthening the "Wheelbarrow" line, insists on a certain looseness, a lack of rigidity which Williams felt Whitman had defined as essential to American poetics. Similarly, the last "incomplete" stanza—a device Williams often resorts to in poems of this period—loosens the poem's formal structure even further, as it opens the poem beyond itself. But Williams's refusal to let this poem stand, finally, as a "figure" for the form he was seeking, his change of the title, indicates that the loosened "Wheelbarrow" stanza is too restrictive. It does not allow enough scope, enough range, for him to accommodate the multiplicity of modern experience within it. What Williams needed to discover, and what he would not discover until the late 1940s, was not only a formal order capable of admitting into itself the multiplicity of modernity, but also one which would not deny, in its repetition over the course of a long poem like *Paterson,* or even in its repetition in a series of unrelated short poems, the sense of chance and surprise that we encounter in the ready-made. Crudely put, the sense of order that Williams discovered in "The Red Wheelbarrow" grows old fast.

NOTES

1. William Carlos Williams, "America, Whitman, and the Art of Poetry," *Poetry Journal* 8 (November 1917): 29–31.

2. William Carlos Williams, "Studiously Unprepared: Notes for Various Talks and Readings, May 1940 to April 1941," Yale MS.

3. Ezra Pound, *Gaudier-Brzeska: A Memoir* (1916; reprint, New York: New Directions, 1970), p. 86.

4. Ibid., p. 89.

5. James Guimond, "After Imagism," *Ohio Review* 15 (Fall 1973): 5. Guimond quotes Bly's statement (p. 24).

6. Abraham A. Davidson, "John Marin: A Dynamism Codified," *Artforum* 9 (April 1971): 37.

7. William Carlos Williams, "A Note on Poetry," *Oxford Anthology of American Literature,* ed. William Rose Benét and Norman Holmes Pearson (New York: Oxford University Press, 1938), p. 1313.

8. Paul Strand, "Photography," *Camera Work* 49/50 (June 1917): 4.

9. Quoted in Dorothy Norman, *Alfred Stieglitz: An American Seer* (New York: Random House, 1973), p. 76.

10. Charles Sheeler, "Notes on an Exhibition of Greek Art," reprinted in National Collection of Fine Arts, *Charles Sheeler* (Washington: Smithsonian Institution Press, 1968), p. 94.

11. Quoted in Constance Rourke, *Charles Sheeler: Artist in the American Tradition* (New York: Harcourt, Brace, 1938), p. 143.

12. Marius de Zayas, "Photography and Artistic-Photography," *Camera Work* 42/43 (April-July 1913): 13.

13. Paul Strand, "Photography," p. 3.

14. Quoted in Norman, *Alfred Stieglitz,* p. 161.

15. Alfred Stieglitz, "Our Illustrations," *Camera Work* 49/50 (June 1917): 36.

16. Quoted in Norman, *Alfred Stieglitz,* p. 161.

17. William C. Seitz, *The Art of Assemblage* (New York: Museum of Modern Art, 1961), pp. 73–74.

18. Donald B. Kuspit, "Individual and Mass Identity in Urban Art: The New York Case," *Art in America* 65 (September-October 1977): 68.

19. Ibid.

20. Quoted in Norman, *Alfred Stieglitz,* pp. 39, 45.

21. Marius de Zayas, "From *291—July-August* Number, 1915," *Camera Work* 48 (October 1916): 69.

22. John Marin, introduction to the Marin Exhibition, Photo-Succession Gallery, 1913, reprinted in *Camera Work* 42/43 (April-July 1913): 18.

23. John Grierson, "Metropolitan," *Films* 1 (1939), reprinted in *Grierson on Documentary Art,* ed. Forsyth Hardy (Berkeley: University of California Press, 1966), p. 219.

24. In *Hieroglyphics,* Dijkstra says (p. 191) that "Classic Scene" is based on Sheeler's 1931 *Classic Landscape.* As with his discussion of "The Rose" and *Roses,* he offers no evidence. Common sense would seem to indicate otherwise. In Sheeler's painting there is only one large smokestack—not a pair—though seven other small ones do stretch across the background. Nor is there anything resembling a red-brick powerhouse—though perhaps Dijkstra was working with a black-and-white reproduction. If there is any connection to Sheeler's painting at all, it is only in Williams's use of the word "classic" —the irony of which, one imagines, he *might* have borrowed from the painting's title.

25. Williams, "The Great Sex Spiral: A Criticism of Miss Marsden's 'Lingual Psychology,'" *The Egoist* 4 (August 1917): 111.

26. Marius de Zayas, "Femme!" *291* 9 (November 1915).

27. Quoted in Norman, *Alfred Stieglitz,* p. 137.

28. Williams's text was originally illustrated by Romare Bearden's 1947 *Women with an Oracle (RI,* facing page 180). Dijkstra's introduction to *A Recognizable Image* details many connections between "The Great Sex Spiral" and "Woman as Operator."

29. For a comparison of the Demuth and Johns paintings see Harry Geldzahler, "Numbers in Time: Two American Paintings," *Metropolitan Museum of Art Bulletin* 23 (April 1965): 295–99. Michael Crichton's discussion of Johns's *Figure 7* is useful in this context: "Numbers exist only in the imagination. We write them every day, we use them all the time, but they remain abstract in a peculiar way. Johns paints his numbers as if they had some inherent concrete reality—and indeed the very act of painting produces a kind of concrete reality. What is that painting? It is a painting of the number 7, the shape of the numeral, standing without a context. Cézanne painted seven apples; Johns just paints 7. Such lack of context for the 'subject,' the painted figure, makes us acutely aware of the painting itself as a physical object" (*Jasper Johns* [New York: Abrams, 1977], p. 31).

30. Hugh Kenner, *A Homemade World: The American Modernist Writers* (New York: Knopf, 1975), pp. 58–60.

31. Marcel Duchamp, "The Richard Mutt Case," *The Blind Man* 2 (May 1917): 5.

32. J. Hillis Miller's insistence on Williams's leap into things and consequent avoidance of metaphor causes him to read this poem as straight description, which diminishes the poem's accomplishment considerably. See *Poets of Reality,* pp. 345–47.

33. *Galaxy: An Anthology,* ed. Beatrix Reynolds and James Gabelle (Ridgefield, N.J.: Gayren Press, 1934), p. 98.

CHAPTER THREE

Shaping the Poem

If the formal discoveries of "The Red Wheelbarrow" finally proved relatively useless to Williams, the poem nonetheless established a direction in which his poetics would move for over a quarter-century. Before *Spring and All* virtually no poems in the Williams canon have a consistent stanzaic arrangement.[1] And although other poems in *Spring and All* possess recognizable and consistent formal patterning, none possesses quite the combination of formal order together with an almost total lack of the poet's subjective presence which characterizes the "Wheelbarrow." However, many later poems combine precisely its sense of formal design with its brand of objective reportage. Beginning with *Collected Poems 1921–1931,* the volume of poems which Louis Zukofsky edited for the Objectivist Press, and continuing through to the late 1940s, virtually every Williams poem (barring those written before 1928) which has a recognizable stanzaic pattern is an objective description of reality. This includes most of the poems under three pages in *An Early Martyr* (1935), *Adam and Eve and the City* (1936), *The Broken Span* (1941), *The Wedge* (1944), and *The Clouds* (1948). In the *Autobiography* Williams says of his work during this period: "The poem being an object (like a symphony or a cubist painting) it must be the purpose of the poet to make of his words a new form: to invent, that is, an object consonant with his day. This was what we wished to imply by Objectivism, an antidote, in a sense, to the bare image haphazardly presented in loose verse" (*A,* 265). Louis Zukofsky, editor of the 1931 "Objectivist" number of *Poetry,* had tied the "movement" from the outset to photography: "An Objective: (Optics)—The lens bringing the rays from an object to a focus," the number began.[2] Like photography, the objectivist poem is not merely a plain presentation of the facts, but the facts ordered, designed, raised out of the banal and into the realm of art. This formal imperative, which is at the heart of objectivism but is often ignored, is probably nowhere more clearly stated than in Williams's brief definition of the movement written in the early 1960s for the *Princeton Encyclopedia of Poetry and Poetics:* "[Objectivism] recognizes the poem with a special eye to its structural aspect, how it has been constructed. . . . The mind rather than the unsupported eye entered the picture."[3] In the end, the aims of objectivism are not much different from what Williams had called for in the 1917 "America, Whitman, and the Art of Poetry." But the objectivists did champion and encourage in Williams a distinct kind of poem. The bulk of Williams's work which Zukofsky included in the 1932 *"Objectivists" Anthology* is of the patterned variety. The earliest poem Zukofsky published was "To Elsie," from *Spring and All,* which with "The Red Wheelbarrow" is one of the most formally consistent poems in that volume.

This is not to say, of course, that either "The Red Wheelbarrow" or "To Elsie" or any subsequent patterned poem is purely objective. On the contrary, we are always aware of the subjective vision which sees and records these objective facts. More important, we witness that subjectivity's very real manifestation, as Williams's *Encyclopedia* definition states, in the order the poem achieves. But it is to say, as a general rule, that almost every time Williams abandons objective description—whenever the first person, singular or plural, appears in a poem after the late 1920s—the poem possesses no consistent stanzaic pattern. These unpatterned, more personal poems are generally longer, more emotional, and less controlled than the patterned objective ones, and include the likes of "Adam" (about Williams's father), "Eve" (about his mother), "The Crimson Cyclamen" (written in memory of Demuth), "Elegy for D. H. Lawrence," "To All Gentleness," "The Forgotten City," "To Ford Madox Ford in Heaven," and others in this general vein. Even in a number of shorter poems the poet's overt presence seems to offset the necessity of consistently patterned stanzas. "To a Wood Thrush" (*CEP*, 367), the opening poem in *Adam and Eve and the City*, begins by describing, in a five-line stanza, the wood thrush's call. Then it shifts from description, speaks in a second five-line stanza of the difficulty of writing about anything, and concludes with this disjointed four-liner:

> What can I say?
> Vistas
> of delight waking suddenly
> before a cheated world.

Any sense of stanzaic pattern that the first two stanzas might have established is reversed by the last. The divorce of the writing from the vision seems to justify the lack of form. Similarly, "The Last Turn" (*CLP*, 44) is one continuous eighteen-line poem which, as the final poem in *The Broken Span* (1941), images the lack of a bridge between the chaotic world and the ordering mind. A description of the scene at the corner of 53rd Street and Eighth Avenue in New York on a night which seems to echo the atmosphere of "The Great Figure," the poem begins with the expletive "Then see it!" But no sense of the formal clarity that *seeing* generally precipitates in Williams's work, and certainly no formal pattern, is developed. We see instead only "the cross lights echoing the/ crazy weave of the breaking mind." The chaos of the world is not ordered by the imagination, merely recorded by it: "the whole [scene is] one/ jittering direction made of all/ directions spelling the inexplicable." But what is explicable is the nature of the poet's frustration. He finds the ordering mind—"the fury of/ our concepts"—pitted against "the genius of a world" which is "artless but supreme," and this sudden insight into the inevitable discord between mind and world, order and fact, separates him from much of his own work, those poems in which the artless world is formally elevated to art.

One way to approach the poetry of Williams's middle years is to recognize that there are two kinds of poems, one visionary and one visual. To return to and paraphrase the *Autobiography's* definition of objectivism, whenever Williams presents us with what he calls the "bare image," he usually does so in a very strict verse form. But whenever that bare image is graced by his subjective presence, he seems more comfortable with a "loose verse form" which the objectivists (and he himself) often found inadequate. The "loose" form is visionary; the "strict" form is visual. I doubt that Williams was ever aware that his verse could be categorized in this way (certainly the exceptions to the rule indicate that he wasn't particularly), but it is important to note that the two types of poems are based upon competing aesthetic assumptions. That is, their simultaneous occurrence in the body of Williams's work belies a fundamental aesthetic inconsistency. On the one hand, he would have it that the mind represents itself by the abstract designs it discovers or creates, by the order it imposes on reality. On the other hand, whenever his poems are most clearly about the mind, they tend to be disorderly. In one kind of poem the imagination is defined as the place from which form and order spring; in the other, especially in contrast to the first, the imagination seems to be disorder's natural home.

There are, then, really two "imaginations" at work in Williams's poetics. The first is what he would himself see as a sort of *universal artist's* imagination, that imagination which throughout history and across time has always remade the world into a thing of beauty and order. The second might be called the *modern's* imagination, a direct function of Williams's own history and time, of contemporary experience in all its multiplicity and confusion. This second "imagination" imitates the day, rather than transcending it. That is, the modern's imagination is mimetic while the artist's is not: the "loose" forms it discovers are *organically* derived from the very "looseness" of experience itself. The forms in which the artist's imagination represents itself, however, are *artificial* in the best sense of the word, strictly structured and designed.

The resolution of this tension within Williams's aesthetic probably begins in his concern for what he always called "the American idiom." To borrow a phrase from the aesthetics of photography, Williams resorts again and again in his poetry to the "straight" presentation of the American speech act. It is as if, instead of using a camera in order to record empirically the objects of the American scene, Williams uses a tape recorder to record empirically the American idiom. His original objective seems more analytic than synthetic: to reveal the formal character of the "local" or individual utterance, to reveal the universal in the local, the abstract design in the particular "fact" of experience. At the conclusion of "Sunday" (*CEP*, 109–10), Williams records what he can hear of a conversation:

> "Over Labor Day they'll
> be gone"
> "Jersey City, he's the
> engineer—" "Ya"
> "Being on the Erie R.R.
> is quite convenient"
>
> "No, I think they're—"
> "I think she is. I think—"
> "German-American"
> "Of course the Govern—"

These voices are part of the "sounds" which make up the day, the experience: the "clatter of metal in a pan," "a splash of water," the "clap of a door," and the "scrape of a chair/ clickaty tee." Clatter, splash, clap, clickaty tee, these voices describe "a tune nameless as Time," and a tune as American as the Sunday comics.

But the American idiom does not become poetry simply by virtue of the fact that it "sounds." There is a difference between mere saying and poetic saying. The question becomes, By what operation—by discovering form *in* the world or by imposing form *upon* it—is *saying* elevated to the *poetic?* The question, in terms of Williams's own poetry, is, By what right does his famous note apologizing for eating the plums become something more than a note? By what right does something called "This Is Just to Say" (*CEP*, 354) become a poem?[4] In the end, Williams had to ask himself this same question when he decided to write poetry about the anti-poetic matter of the city. And the answer is the same: *Unless it is formed, it is not poetry.* The poem's intrinsic necessity is to compose the landscape or the idiom it records.

As early as "America, Whitman, and the Art of Poetry," Williams had recognized that although the poem would be constructed of "all temperaments, all phases of our environment, physical as well as spiritual" (as Whitman's was), it equally "must be governed," and it was in the discovery of this governing principle that the poem and America would be "rebuilt." In the 1930s and 1940s in the poems which empirically record the American idiom as it is spoken—in the four separate "Detail" poems (*CEP*, 427–28), in "At the Bar," (*CEP*, 431), in "To Greet a Letter Carrier" (*CEP*, 432), and in "Après le Bain" (*CLP*, 196)—Williams discovered what he believed this governing principle to be. In the first place, these poems exist in a poetic space which isolates them from and raises them above normal discourse. Selected from the discourse of daily activity, they have been framed and given a transcendent presence; that is, their constitution and composition as poems implies that they have crossed a threshold of discontinuity which separates them from "normal" utterance. Thus, when we confront this "Detail," two separate readings are provoked:

> Doc, I bin lookin' for you
> I owe you two bucks.
>
> How you doin'?
>
> Fine. When I get it
> I'll bring it up to you.
>   (*CEP*, 427)

In the first place, we accept the poem for what it is—a mildly humorous anecdote which in some way epitomizes a country doctor's relationship with his patients. But there is a certain urge to take things further than this. As a representative "detail" from the doctor's experience, the poem establishes the ground for an encounter between competing cultural values, between, for instance, "How you doin'?" uttered as a commonplace and meaningless greeting and as the expression of a doctor's professional concern. In short, the poem becomes a small treatise on the way in which the culture's preoccupation with money and credit drains human feeling from human discourse. But at this point the reading begins to seem strained, to reach beyond the simplicity of the poem and to elevate it in a way that is antagonistic to its own matter-of-factness. Poems like this "Detail" in fact call to task our literary competence, the assumptions about reading poetry which we bring to the poem. In this case, in order to regard Williams's dialogue as a poem we have decided that it is "representative" of a general cultural problem. We have taken it symbolically. We have done this in order to allow ourselves to accept Williams's implicit assumption that this "Detail" is a poem. Nevertheless, the poem's matter-of-factness draws attention to the self-conscious reading we have brought to it, and this self-consciousness of our own activity as readers, our own symbol-mongering, provides the framework for a second, perhaps more satisfactory reading. The poem, in effect, asks why it is a poem. The inescapable answer is that it is a poem because it is structured like a poem. It exists in poetic space.[5]

This second "reading" is not as simple as it might at first sound, for it implies that *all* poems must exist in a structured space. More specifically, it defines what Williams considered to be the inadequacy of his "loose" visionary poems: they are not fully designed and composed. Furthermore, the reading raises questions about the privileges language as poetry holds over language as speech. Although this poem—like all poems—is made of language, language is not poetry unless it occurs in poetic space. The poem posits all language as *potential* language for poetry. In the poem "Fragment" (*CEP*, 453), itself a recorded conversation, Williams explains what his records of conversation accomplish:

> My God, Bill, what have you done?
>
> What do you think I've done? I've
> opened up the world.
>
> Where did you get them? Marvellous
> beautiful!
>
> Where does all snot come from? Under
> the nose,
>
> Yea-uh?
>
> —the gutter, where everything comes
> from, the manure heap.

Under our noses, in the very coarseness of our expression, lies what Williams later called, in *Paterson,* "a world unsuspected." We can leave the American idiom in "the gutter," as part of "the manure heap," or we can elevate it to poetry. As poetry it becomes "marvellous/ beautiful," and in choosing to elevate the idiom to poetry Williams has in fact "opened up the world."

More important, the "Detail" poems underscore the discontinuity between language (mere saying) and poetry (poetic saying), that is, a discontinuity between *utterance* and *utterance given the form of poetry.* If we take the poem as a representation of this discontinuity, the inadequacy of our first symbolic "reading" is exposed. For our first reading depends, like utterance, on the establishment of a limiting context, an implicit narrative or life, in order to reveal its signification. The idea that the poem is a "detail" provokes this contextual effort, the urge to see it as a part of a larger experience. However, this effort to discover a context in which to place the poem denies the poem's integrity. The idea that the poem is a poem, above and beyond the fact that it is a detail, establishes it as a *text* independent of the necessity for a specific *context.* Williams calls these lines simply "Poem" —as opposed to say, "The Cat"—in order to make the same point:

> As the cat
> climbed over
> the top of
>
> the jamcloset
> first the right
> forefoot
>
> carefully
> then the hind
> stepped down
>
> into the pit of
> the empty
> flowerpot
>   (*CEP,* 340)

These lines are not mere description. They are a "Poem." Their formal presentation elevates them to the world of poetry.

The poem's formal dimension is, in fact, made up of two more or less independent but simultaneous operations, one aural and the other visual. The first is the result of a careful manipulation of certain consonants which wind very precisely through the poem—*c, f, t,* and *p* particularly. The precision of this sound pattern is emphasized by the concentration of these aspirated consonants in the single stressed word of a given line—"cat," "top," "pit," and "empty," for instance. The net result is that in describing the careful movement of the cat, the poem seems to be describing its own purposeful aural movement as well.

This is an almost classic example of organic form, but it does not fully describe all the formal features of the poem. Consider also its stanzaic pattern. The logic of the stanza breaks seems, in fact, to be arbitrary and mechanical, a function of Williams's effort to make the poem recognizably a poem by imposing upon it an orderly stanzaic arrangement, which possesses no particular thematic, grammatical, or aural logic and which is wholly visual. In an interview with Mike Wallace of CBS which he incorporates into *Paterson*, Book Five, Williams rejects a poem by e e cummings as poetry because he "cant understand it." The poem reads:

> (im)c-a-t-(mo)
> b,i;l:e
>
> FallleA
> ps!fl
> OattumblI
>
> sh?dr
> IftwhirlF
> (Ul) (lY)
> &&&
> (*P*, 224)

But cummings is demonstrating in a more radical way what Williams's "Poem" demonstrates. The poem, deciphered, reads: "I'm cat, mobile, fall, leaps, float, tumblish, drift, whirl, fully, etc." Cummings is drawing attention to the difference his poem's typograpy—its visual presentation—makes in our ability to understand even simple language. The poem possesses the power to transform language. In cummings's poem language has nearly been destroyed, but it *has been changed,* just as Williams insists that language "must change . . . reappear in another form, to remain permanent" (*SE,* 208). The privilege of poetic activity is that it draws attention to itself, to its form, to the fact that a "Poem" has been made, to the discontinuity between undifferentiated space and poetic space.

II

Poetic space, in short, is a visual as well as an aural space. Lifting the American idiom into the poem involves more than simply recording, as in the poem "Sunday," the idiom's sounds. They must be recorded in such a way that they are recognizably poeticized. In an undated and unpublished manuscript, Williams addressed the issue directly:

> There are various forms of poetry
> and one of them is the lovely sound
> of words tuned skillfully to please
> the ear as another, requiring less
> tuneful handling, gives itself to
> holding before the eye a well imagined
> image. Neither is complete without
> the other, it may be said, in a full
> work. But the two are the principal
> forms to be borne well in mind in
> all major compositions. When the eye
> can no longer delineate or bear the
> brunt of the thought and the intelligence
> goes off into regions where sight
> cannot follow the ear begins its reign.[6]

The phrase "a well imagined/ image" seems to indicate that Williams is approaching the visual dimension of the poem in close to imagist terms, as merely the poem's description of an imaginative reality. In addition, he admits that aural poems (such as his own first-person poems of the objectivist period) like to go "off into regions where sight/ cannot follow," though he does seem to assume, as the objectivists did, the priority of the visual, indicating that only after the eye fails does the ear's way of ordering language need to establish itself. But that he is willing to differentiate between visual and aural poetries is important in itself, for it indicates that he is in the process of developing a poetic structure that differs fundamentally from traditional structures dependent on meter or rhyme, structures where the ear has always dominated the eye.

In his little-known but very interesting study of inscription, *Visible Words,* John Sparrow has argued that inscription—on tombstones, statues, buildings, and title pages—developed in the seventeenth century into a full-fledged literary genre which insisted that "visual form should be an essential constituent" of literary art. Sparrow's definition of inscription seems to suit Williams's poetry precisely: "a text composed with a view to its being presented in lines of different lengths, the lineation contributing to or enhancing the meanings, so that someone who does not see it, actually or in his mind's eye, but only hears it read aloud misses something of the intended effect."[7] Like the literary inscription, Williams's poetry must be read with the eye. Otherwise our sense of its structure—which is to say its stature as poetry —is jeopardized. By the time of the publication of *Collected Poems* (1938), Williams had begun to sense how important a poem's look on the page was to his poetics:

> The *Collected Poems* gave me the whole picture, all I had gone through technically to learn about the making of a poem. I could look at the poems as they lay before me. I could reject the looseness of the free verse. Free verse wasn't verse at all to me. All art is orderly. . . . From the beginning I knew that the American language must shape the pattern; later I rejected the word language and spoke of the American idiom—this was a better word than language, less academic, more identified with speech. As I went through the poems I noticed many brief poems, always arranged in couplet or quatrain form. I noticed also that I was peculiarly fascinated by another pattern: the dividing of the little paragraphs in lines of three. I remembered writing several poems as quatrains at first, then in the normal process of concentrating the poem, getting rid of redundancies in the line—and in the attempt to make it go faster—the quatrain changed into a three line stanza, or a five line stanza became a quatrain, as in:

The Nightingales

Original Version	*Revised Version*
My shoes as I lean	My shoes as I lean
unlacing them	unlacing them
stand out upon	stand out upon
flat worsted flowers	flat worsted flowers
under my feet	
Nimbly the shadows	Nimbly the shadows
of my fingers play	of my fingers play
unlacing	unlacing
over shoes and flowers.	over shoes and flowers.

See how much better it conforms to the page, how much better it looks? (*IWWP*, 65–66)

Although Williams's revision is an attempt to get "rid of redundancies in the line" in order to concentrate on the poem's particular details, his awareness that the revised version "looks" better has nothing to do either with the poem's subject matter or with its aural dimension (though the revision does, of course, emphasize certain verbal repetitions). The abstract form the poem assumes results from the imposition of stanzaic form upon the anarchy of the "speaking" (or mere "saying," in the American idiom) which it records.

Williams's accidental discovery of a consistent visual pattern in so many of the shorter pieces in *Collected Poems* caused many problems for him, especially in the longer poems he was more and more disposed to write in his later years. The difficulties are nowhere more apparent than in the 1948 poem "Two Pendants: for the Ears" (*CLP*, 214–29). The poem has been nicely analyzed by Neil Myers, who notes that Williams's determination "to make the language/ record it [the particularity of experience]/ facet to facet" is the source, in this poem at least, of Williams's despair.[8] The only thing Myers fails to take into account is Williams's desire to design these details formally, a desire which Williams sees as the source of his salvation. If, as Myers notes and the epigraph to the poem's first section suggests, "the particulars of morning are more to be desired than night's vague images," the particulars of morning happen to be the particulars of his mother's death and are a nightmare in themselves. The poem is founded in crisis, the crisis of an Easter week in which the despair of Williams's dying mother becomes the poet's own:

> Don't go. I am unhappy.
> About what? I said.
> About what is what.

Williams cannot make "what is what" disappear, just as he cannot respond adequately to his mother's plea:

> Can't you give me
> something to make me disappear
> completely, said she sobbing—but
> completely!
>
> No I can't do that
> Sweetheart (You God damned belittling
> fool, said I to myself)

The poem's first nightmare, the night-vision of the crowd huddled underground in terror of the killer tiger, is a scene in which Williams can "make out nothing clearly" and so is "helpless." This "dream" is supplanted by the view from Williams's bathroom window, a view in which "everything is clear," a view of his garden "marked (plotted) by the squares/ and oblongs of the flower beds" where the flowers will eventually blossom "in rows/ irregularly." The first section concludes with the reassuring and redeeming recognition of "the characteristic shape" of a "battered watering can." When Williams turns, in the second section, "Elena," to a recording of the conversation surrounding his mother's nightmarish death, the reassuring vision of "characteristic shape" is lost beneath the weight of the poem's chaotic record of "speaking." But the second section begins to look, on the page, like the garden Williams has described: "squares/ and oblongs . . . in rows, irregularly." The implication, certainly justified by the poem's Easter setting, is that if Williams could image some "characteristic shape" as his record of "what is what," then he might rescue the scene from its apparent chaos.

One of the most interesting things about "Two Pendants" is that the notion of form it advances is essentially *organicist*, as the garden metaphor implies, but Williams's inability to achieve any finally "characteristic shape" in the "Elena" section accounts for the undeniable despair of the poem as a whole, its dominating nightmare quality. If the poem's lines fall into "rows/ irregularly," the oblongs and squares which spatially and visually compose the "Elena" section are themselves irregular. The poem possesses no reassuring and characteristic stanzaic shape—anything which, in the midst of its recording of the chaotic and particular details of morning, will act as a counterpoint to the chaos itself. Williams has made a poem which, as the title implies, is solely "for the ears." Interestingly enough, the one moment when Williams finds himself at ease in the poem is that moment when he *looks* out the window of his bathroom and sees *shapes,* forms, design. "Overlooking the/ garden" he no longer can "hear" the world's "howls." His lines succeed in recording the irregular pattern of aural speech. His stanza must reflect a regular spatial shape which counterpoints the chaos of speech. In other words, he must discover a visual form which makes an ordered poetic saying out of the irregularity of *mere* saying, simultaneously reflecting and recording both.

The poetic form by which Williams synthesized visual order and aural irregularity is the generally triadic variable foot of his late poetry. As he would describe it in 1946, it is based on "a line as loose as Whitman's, but *measured* as his was not."[9] The inspiration for the triadic variable foot can be seen to originate both in the ordered stanzaic form of the brief poems and in the stanzaic arrangement, usually much looser, of poems which "record the language" like the "Detail" poems or the "Elena" section of "Two Pendants." The triadic variable foot is a formal synthesis of both. The brief poems arranged in two-, three-, or four-line stanzas have the advantage of "looking" like poetry. The poems that record the language "facet to facet" are patterns "shaped" by the American idiom. To the eye they appear much looser, their stanzaic pattern determined usually by the unit of statement; that is, a stanza is a unit of speech, the record of a complete utterance. The variable foot is visually "mechanical" or "abstract"; it is aurally organic. It achieves overall visual orderliness while at the same time it allows the American idiom to determine the more or less "loose" shape of the individual lines.

Williams described the 1930s as "a time when I was working hard for order, searching for a form for the stanzas, making them little units, regular, orderly. The poem 'Fine Work with Pitch and Copper' is really telling about my struggled with verse" (*IWWP*, 57). The poem is literally about roofing a house. Before the "flat roof" of the house can be graveled, the top edge of the masonry wall, the "coping," must be edged with pitch and copper in order to waterproof the roof. In other words, the roof must be framed before "the sacks/ of sifted stone" can be "opened and strewn." If this necessity of house-making is extended to poem-making, Williams is positing that the poem must be *framed*, that this frame must be composed of regular and *measured* units (like "the copper in eight/ foot strips"), and that each unit must be "beaten lengthwise" so that when the poet/ carpenter "runs his eye along it" its shape will fit into the final pattern (*CEP*, 368). Similarly, the gravel, the material of which the roof/poem will be made, must rest in the sacks until the framing pattern is completed.

"Fine Work with Pitch and Cooper" "looks" like a poem, just as a house, before its roofing is completed, looks like a house. Nevertheless, the poem implies that "the fine work" of measuring the line awaits completion. Williams had recognized the importance of the overall frame or order at least as early as "The Red Wheelbarrow," where the poem's formal organization determines the importance we attach to it, drawing our attention to verbal relationships we might otherwise ignore. The rationale for the stanza divisions in "The Red Wheelbarrow" is clearly based on the idea of "phrase"; the second line of each stanza is the word which completes the phrase and upon which the phrase depends. In effect, this pattern is achieved through a careful consideration of the inherent shape of the "American idiom." When Williams attempts empirically to "record" the language "facet to facet" in later poems, however, the characteristic and orderly shape achieved in "The Red Wheelbarrow" stanza is generally lost. In "Two Pendants," for instance, the stanza indicates, as in the paragraphing of dialogue in prose, simply who is speaking. The stanza is one line or many, depending upon the length of the particular speech act Williams records. The stanza is literally "beaten lengthwise." Compared to the stanzaic arrangement of "Two Pendants," the ordered stanzaic arrangement of "The Red Wheelbarrow" seems gratuitous: "The Red Wheelbarrow" is ordered by the happy coincidence that all four "phrases" happen to be more or less the same length, but the "phrases" which make up the American idiom empirically recorded "facet to facet" simply do not reflect any such regular order.

The idea that utterance possesses length, however variably, is a notion that allows Williams finally to order what appears impossible to order. For the idea of length implies that empirical measurement is taking place. "Measure served us as the key," he would write in 1955. But measure is complicated by the mutability and ambiguity of existence: "How can we accept Einstein's theory of relativity, affecting our very conception of the heavens about us of which poets write so much, without incorporating its essential fact—the relativity of measurements—into our own category of activity: the poem" (SE, 283). In order to deal adequately with his world, Williams needs "a relatively stable foot, not a rigid one" (SE, 340). Each line in Williams's later poetry represents, then, a "foot" or a beat, a unit of measure, but one capable of reflecting the essential fact of modern existence—relativity.

He would describe how this unit of measure functions in a 1954 letter to Richard Eberhart:

> If we keep in mind the *tune* which the lines (not necessarily the words) make in our ears, we are ready to proceed. By measure I mean musical pace. . . .
>
> By its *music* shall the best of modern verse be known and *resources* of the music. The refinement of the poem, its subtlety, is not to be known by the elevation of the words but—the words don't so much matter—by the resources of the music.
>
> To give you an example from my own work—not that I know anything about what I have myself written:
>
> (count):—not that I ever count when writing but, at best, the lines must be capable of being counted, that is to say, *measured*—(believe it or not).

—At that I may, half consciously, even count the measure under my breath as I write.—
(approximate example)
  (1) The smell of the heat is boxwood
      (2) when rousing us
         (3) a movement of the air
  (4) stirs our thoughts
      (5) that had no life in them
         (6) to a life, a life in which
(or)
  (1) Mother of God! Our Lady!
      (2) the heart
         (3) is an unruly master:
  (4) Forgive us our sins
      (5) as we
         (6) forgive
(7) those who have sinned against

Count a single beat to each numeral. You may not agree with
my ear, but that is the way I count the line. Over the whole poem
it gives a pattern to the meter that can be felt as a new measure.
(*SL*, 326–27)

Once again Williams is taking advantage of our literary competence, for his "new measure" defies all traditional metrical
exegesis.[10] Seeking in the poem a metric which is superficially
absent, we are forced to discover a new concept of meter. Any
given line possesses its own particular rhythm but this rhythm
can in no way be generalized into a traditional metric. The only
consistent aspect to Williams's "metric" is metrical inconsistency. On the other hand, as the last sentence of the Eberhart
letter suggests, "over the whole poem" we can feel a "meter,"
the "new measure." Williams creates a sense of consistency by
the visual pattern of repetition into which he arranges his variable lines. Although this arrangement generally involves three-
stepped groups, the differing formal arrangements of the poems
which make up the late "Some Simple Measures in the American
Idiom and the Variable Foot" (*PB*, 47–52) reveal that any pattern will do. What is important is that *in pattern* the line, or
variable foot, does in fact relinquish to the larger visual pattern

whatever traditional metric or seeming lack of metric it might possess, and this pattern in turn enforces the idea that each line is *equal*—whatever its length—to the others in the poem. This pattern, despite Williams's claim that his line records some vaguely defined *music,* is a visual pattern, not an aural one. That is, his "rhythm" is the result of the eye's following a repeated pattern—"rhythm," then, in painting's sense of the word. Williams knew this and in fact acknowledged the visual source of his rhythm on several occasions. As early as 1940 he told an audience at Cooper Union that measure must be based on a *"visual* division of the parts of the poem into units."[11] And, in the spring of 1962, discussing "The Descent" (*PB,* 73–74)— which Williams first published as a separate poem and then interpolated into *Paterson,* and which he always cited as the first example of the variable foot in his poetry—Stanley Koehler said to Williams: "The appearance of this poem on the page suggests you were conscious of it as a thing—something for the eye." Williams replied: "Yes, very good. I was conscious of making it even. I wanted it to be read regularly. . . . The total effect is very important."[12] In essence, the overall effect of the poem's visual *pattern of repetition* that this shape establishes makes each line, over the whole poem, *seem* "a single beat"— that is, a single move of the eye, and thus a single visual unit equal to the other units (or lines) of the poem.

The device of the variable foot in pattern solves a number of problems for Williams. Since each "foot" is variable, the line length can legitimately derive from the American idiom. Each line can be an empirical and realistic record of that idiom and need not distort it. When the line is put in pattern with other lines, however, its irregularity becomes an aspect of a larger orderliness, an abstraction. This larger order in no way denies the individual line's inherent disorder. Both order and disorder, abstraction and realism, occur simultaneously. The poem is a conversation between reality and abstraction and is the sign of their inevitable interaction. The poem is a *double action* in which the demands of reality and the demands of the abstracting mind act "separately in unison." It insists on the heterogeneity of its considered parts.

In the end, the patterned variable foot represents the revolution in poetic form, and therefore in turn poetic content, which in 1939 Williams had seen as an absolute necessity:

> The mutability of the truth, Ibsen said it. Jefferson said it. We should have a revolution of some sort in America every ten years. The truth has to be redressed, re-examined, reaffirmed in a new mode. There has to be new poetry. But the thing is that the change, the greater material, the altered structure of the inevitable revolution must be *in* the poem, in it. Made of it. It must shine in the structural body of it. (*SE*, 217)

Paterson is the embodiment of this revolution. Its "double action" is asserted at the outset of its preface:

> To make a start,
> out of particulars
> and make them general, rolling
> up the sum

it opens (*P*, 3), asserting the importance of beginning in reality, in analysis. But a few lines later Williams asserts the value of beginning in abstraction—"from mathematics to particulars" (*P*, 5)—and both are the way "to Paterson"

>   it can't be
> otherwise—an
> interpenetration, both ways. Rolling
> up! obverse, reverse;
> the drunk the sober; the illustrious
> the gross; one.

Paterson is an "interpenetration, both ways," a conversation between abstraction and reality. The poem even represents the "ten years" revolution which Williams believed necessary in America. Initially conceived as a four-part narrative—"I took the river as it followed its course down to the sea. . . . Each Part of the poem was planned as unit complete in itself, reporting the progress of the river" (*IWWP*, 73)—the first part was published in 1946 and the next three soon followed. But in 1958 *Paterson* revolted against itself: a fifth book appeared, shattering this narrative structure completely. First, however, in *Paterson*, Book Two, Williams discovered the variable foot, the device which would free him to realize in "the structural body" of the poem "the mutability of truth." In a moment of despair, at a moment when it seems that all a man can do is "chatter of his doom," these lines and the pattern which they anticipate provoke "a reversal/ of despair":

> No defeat is made up entirely of defeat—since
> the world it opens is always a place
> > formerly
> > > unsuspected. A
> world lost
> > a world unsuspected
> > > beckons to new places
> > > > (P, 78)

"Now I had it," Williams would later say of these lines, "a sea change" (*IWWP*, 83). Out of a world in which all the products of humanity—including the poem—seem destined for defeat, an awakening is promised, an awakening out of which Williams would finally fashion a consistent aesthetic vision.

NOTES

1. What appears to be an exception to this occurs in the *Collected Earlier Poems,* "The Nightingales" (*CEP,* 224) in *Sour Grapes.* But Williams revised the poem to give it stanzaic consistency for his *Collected Poems* (1938). This revision is discussed later in the chapter.

2. Louis Zukofsky, "Program: 'Objectivists' 1931," *Poetry* 37 (February 1931): 268.

3. *Princeton Encyclopedia of Poetry and Poetics,* ed. Alex Preminger (Princeton: Princeton University Press, 1965), p. 582.

4. Charles Altieri has addressed these questions in his "Presence and Reference in a Literary Text: The Example of Williams' 'This Is Just to Say,'" *Critical Inquiry* 5 (Spring 1979): 489–510. Many of his conclusions are similar to those I arrive at here: "Williams' poem, after all, is only just saying, but because it is free form rhetoric and forces the poet's creative energies into structurally measuring the experience, it may be the only way poetry can speak justly" (p. 507). A different, somewhat clearer version of this essay, entitled "A Test Case of Action Description: Interpreting Williams' 'This Is Just to Say,'" has since appeared in Altieri's *Act & Quality: A Theory of Literary Meaning and Humanistic Understanding* (Amherst: University of Massachusetts Press, 1981), pp. 160–75. Altieri's revision—and its strategic

place in *Act & Quality* as whole—has important bearing on the argument of my concluding chapter.

5. Again, the logic of my argument here and the logic of Altieri's analysis of "This Is Just to Say" are extremely close. Both of us see the poem as the site of a kind of dialectical play among possible readings which test (though they do not undermine) our competence to assess and value utterances. Though Altieri and I agree that the poem's "structural patterns" and "perspicuous organization" elevate the "saying" of these utterances to poetry, I mean something far more particular by "pattern" and "organization" than Altieri does (see *Act & Quality,* pp. 169–70).

What I am arguing here is essentially a radicalization (or extreme simplification) of what Northrop Frye, in the introduction to the fourth essay of the *Anatomy of Criticism: Four Essays* (Princeton: Princeton University Press, 1957), calls the "radical of presentation," that is, the way in which a text formally announces how it is to be taken. Frye argues that this "radical of presentation" is the basis of generic distinctions between dramatic, epic, and lyric modes, and that it announces "the conditions established between the poet and his public" (p. 247). Refusing to assume "poetry" as a given, Williams goes one step further and points to the "radical of presentation" which announces poetry in the first place: the way in which the recognizability of his (printed) text as poetry—its look on the page—distinguishes it from speech.

6. "There are various forms of poetry," Buffalo MS.

7. John Sparrow, *Visible Words: A Study of Inscriptions in and as Books and Works of Art* (Cambridge: Cambridge University Press, 1969), pp. 141, 5.

8. Neil Myers, "Williams' 'Two Pendants: for the Ears,'" *Journal of Modern Literature* 1 (May 1971): 477–492.

9. William Carlos Williams, preface, *Quarterly Review of Literature* 2 (1946): 349.

10. The frustrations inherent in any attempt to discover traditional metric patterns in Williams's poetry can best be seen in the section devoted to Williams in Harvey Gross's *Sound and Form in Modern Poetry: A Study of Prosody from Thomas Hardy to Robert Lowell* (Ann Arbor: University of Michigan Press, 1968). Gross begins by noting that "nothing, and certainly nothing in the way of a deliberate metric, seems to intervene between us and the sensibility of this extraordinary man" (p. 117). Gross, however, is so determined to discover some semblance of traditional prosody in Williams's work that he finally analyzes "The Yachts" (*CEP,* 106–7) at length. Discovering "a more conventional line" in this poem, he claims that it "ranks with the best poems of our age" largely, perhaps exclusively, because it possesses "a passionately well-ordered metric" (pp. 121–22). "The

Yachts" is among the most atypical of Williams's efforts. In fact, it misrepresents him. It cannot be overemphasized that while Williams's poetry is not traditional, it is nonetheless deliberate and well ordered.

11. Quoted from Williams's "Notes" for a talk and reading given at Cooper Union, 12 April 1940, in Paul Mariani, *William Carlos Williams: A New World Naked* (New York: McGraw-Hill, 1981), p. 437.

12. "The Art of Poetry," interview with Stanley Koehler taped in April 1962, published in *Paris Review* 32 (Summer-Fall 1964): 120.

CHAPTER FOUR

Paterson as Collage

Among the manuscripts of *Paterson* at Yale there is a proposed title page which indicates the aesthetic difficulties Williams faced in the poem:

PATERSON

or

ANY/EVERY Place

of sufficient complexity to

require a detailed synthesis of its

apparent multiplicity

Williams seems to be saying here that the city's multiplicity is only "apparent," that it is an illusion. He is proposing that its complexity and multiplicity be subsumed in the singleness of his own all-encompassing synthetic vision. In other words, the initial project of the poem is ameliorative and idealistic. It would end opposition through synthesis. It would make a world which is essentially heterogeneous into one that is homogeneous.

Paterson, as a whole, denies the possibility of ever realizing this dream of synthesis with which Williams apparently began the poem. He speaks of his final refusal of synthesis in a 1951 letter to Marianne Moore about the "failure" of *Paterson:* "If the vaunted purpose of my poem seems to fall apart at the end— it's rather frequent that one has to admit an essential failure. At times there is no other way to assert the truth than by stating our failure to achieve it. If I did not achieve a language I at least stated what I would not say. I would not melt myself into the great universal sea (of love) with all its shapes and colors" (*SL,*

304). While it is clear that he does not consider the first four books of *Paterson* a success, it is equally clear that the achievement of a singleness and unity of visions—"the great universal sea (of love)"—would not have made for its success, either. What the poem proposes instead—despite Williams's original aim—is an aesthetic of heterogeneity.[1] It brings together many things, but it does not propose their subsumption into a single vision. It simply lets them stand together as if the project of the poem is not to end conflict but to begin it, to see what kinds of conflicts its juxtapositions of opposites can generate.

An aesthetic based on heterogeneity has far-reaching implications for the art object. As I have just indicated, it denies the traditional place of unity and synthesis in the work of art and substitutes ambiguity and simultaneity. One way of putting it is to say that an aesthetic of heterogeneity champions Sergei Eisenstein's famous definition of montage: "Montage is conflict. As the basis of every art is conflict (an 'imagist' transformation of the dialectical principle)."[2] Montage is a technique based on linearity and has been treated, for that reason, as analogous to literature. But it seems to me equally useful to approach *Paterson*'s aesthetic of heterogeneity in terms of montage's spatial cousin, collage, especially since Williams's poetic insists on the visual experience of poetic space. Whereas montage exploits opposition and conflict in general across a wide range of both thematic and technical manifestations, collage concentrates its energies on one conflict in particular, a conflict especially relevant to Williams's aesthetics; that is, the tension between art and reality. By bringing "real" material into the art object (ranging from a piece of newsprint in a cubist collage to a freestanding stuffed goat in Robert Rauschenberg's *Monogram),* collage destroys our traditional assumptions about the work of art. Collage turns the space of the art object into an arena of ambiguity. The autonomous existence of the work of art is challenged by the intrusion of the "real" into its space. Conversely, the "real" is metamorphosed—in a manner analogous to Duchamp's metamorphosis of the urinal by placing it in the context of a museum—by its sudden placement in the realm of art. Collage presents us with a space in which the common object, in all its banality, is elevated to the realm of "high art," and "high art," with all its pretension, is relegated to the world of things. In terms of *Paterson*, the waste and junk of which the city is composed, and the newspapers which record the transience of our day-to-day lives, find themselves elevated into the poem. And the poem itself—as the history of its critical reception testifies—finds itself precariously close to losing its distinction as verse. Speaking of the Marcia Nardi letters at the end of Book Two, Randall Jarrell asks in irritation, "What has been done to them to make it possible for us to respond to them as art, not as raw reality?"[3] In terms of collage the answer is obvious: nothing, save their presence in the poem. But Jarrell's question is the very one that Williams hoped his collage of prose and verse would raise.

All of *Paterson*'s prose is extra-artistic; that is, it is "real" material which has originated in another context and which has been brought into the art world by fiat. As early as *Spring and All* Williams had distinguished between prose and poetry in a manner which defines their collision in *Paterson* not only terms of a confrontation of art and reality but, by extension, of the abstract and the concrete as well. Prose is "the exposition of facts," and poetry is "the crystallization of the imagination" (*I*, 140). Book One of *Paterson* takes immediate advantage of this distinction. The sleeping giants, male and female, form the landscape of the city and its pastoral environs:

> Paterson lies in the valley under the Passaic Falls
> its spent waters forming the outline of his back. He
> lies on his right side, head near the thunder
> of the waters filling his dreams!
> (*P*, 6)

> .   .   .   .

> And there, against him, stretches the low mountain.
> The Park's her head, carved, above the Falls, by the quiet
> river; Colored crystals the secret of those rocks;
> farms and ponds, laurel and the temperate wild cactus,
> yellow flowered   .   .   facing him, his
> arm supporting her, by the Valley of the Rocks, asleep.
> (*P*, 8)

This marriage of the prosaic city and the poetic mountain represents the dream of synthesis to which the poem aspires. But the marriage remains a dream. It is a *vision* of synthesis—a creation of art alone—which is juxtaposed to the reality of the people of Paterson. Thus the marriage of the abstract and the concrete—"mathematics" and "particulars"—which the poem's opening lines propose is itself a dreamy abstraction, juxtaposed, in its turn, to the reality of the crowd which Williams calls several times in Book Two "the great beast" (*P*, 46, 55, 67, 80). Significantly, the characteristics of this "great beast" are detailed by the prose fragments which Williams weaves into the poem. The first describes an 1857 mussel hunt, spurred on by David Hower's discovery of two pearls valued at $900 and $2,000 respectively: "The Unios (mussels) at Notch Brook and elsewhere were gathered by the millions and destroyed often with little or no result. A large round pearl, weighing 400 grains which would have been the finest pearl of modern times, was ruined by boiling open the shell" (*P*, 9). The "great beast" is an agent of destruction here. It is antagonistic to the idea of synthesis, destroying the idea of unity (the "Unios"), and it is the ruination of the beautiful. The beast recurs in many other forms. It is seen in the story of the hydrocephalic who lives in Paterson: "This is a monster in human form . . . his face from the upper part of his forehead to the end of his chin, measures *twenty-seven inches* . . . his body is twenty-seven inches in length, his limbs are small and much deformed" (*P*, 10). A great "natural curiosity" of the city, visited even by General Washington, this monster is an image of the people themselves. The "great beast" rises again when the *Bergen Express and Paterson Advertiser*, under the headline "The Monster Taken," devotes half a column to the capture of a sturgeon "seven feet six inches long, and weighing 126 pounds" which had been "pelted with stones by boys until he was exhausted" (*P*, 10–11). Still later there is a long description of a time when a nearby lake was drained and "millions" of fish and eels were carted away to market by the crowd (*P*, 35). There is, perhaps most pathetic of all, the estimation of a man's life and worth represented in the detailed list of Cornelius Doremus's possessions at death, "goods and chattels appraised at $419.58½" (*P*, 34). The dream of the marriage of the landscape's giants is the antithesis of the milling about of the "great beast." The poet's "wonder" at the "great beast" is elicited by deformity and violence—nature and anomalies of nature destroyed by the greedy perversions of human nature. His "wonder" at the sleeping giants is elicited by beauty and love. The one is the reality of the poet's world, the other the abstraction of the poet's dream. One finds its expression in prose, the other in poetry.

Nowhere is this antagonism more pronounced than in the inability of the two sides to communicate with one another, of prose and poetry to come together. The people who inhabit Paterson know that the world of the sleeping giants surrounds them. They express this knowledge in perverted form in the monstrousness of their own activity, their fascination with the "wonder" of the hydrocephalic dwarf or the "miracle" of a lake drained of its water and choked with dead fish. Their activity is a misunderstanding of the sleeping giants' dream. When they do confront the beauty of the giants' world, their language cannot capture it, even if their feeling can. Williams describes the response of one young girl, for instance:

> a willow twig pulled from a low
> leafless bush in full bud in her hand,
> (or eels or a moon!)
> holds it, the gathered spray,
> upright in the air, the pouring air,
> strokes the soft fur—
> > Ain't they beautiful!
>
> > > (*P*, 19)

In *Paterson* the people "walk incommunicado" (*P*, 9), and "they die also/ incommunicado":

> They sink back into the loam
> > crying out
> —you may call it a cry
> that creeps over them, a shiver
> > as they wilt and disappear
>
> > > (*P*, 11)

.   .   .   .

> Life is sweet
> they say: the language!
> —The language
> is divorced from their minds,
> the language . . the language!
>
> (*P*, 12)

The language of the Falls, the language of which the sleeping giants dream, in Williams's early vision is the clue to the existence of a single source of both poetry and prose. "The language" has been lost and is now only dimly intuited by the "great beast" ("Ain't they beautiful") and fervently sought by the poet ("a wonder"). Poetry itself comes closer to recapturing and rearticulating the language lost by the people, but as it does so it loses contact with the people themselves and for that reason fails to capture the original unity of all opposites. "Geeze, Doc, I guess it's all right," says one representative of the "great beast" in Book Three, "but what the hell does it mean?" (*P*, 114).

In the first book, both the desire and the failure of the people to know "the wonder" of the dream of the sleeping giants, the wonder of the language, is epitomized by the death of Sam Patch. Patch was man compulsively drawn to the roar and speech of the Falls, "a famous jumper" (*P*, 16):

> The water pouring still
> from the edge of the rocks, filling
> his ears with its sound, hard to interpret.
> A wonder!
>
> (*P*, 17)

On the day of his leap into the Passaic, he made a short speech: "A speech! What could he say that he must leap so desperately to complete it? And plunged toward the stream below. But instead of descending with a plummet-like fall his body wavered in the air—Speech had failed him. He was confused. The word had been drained of its meaning" (*P*, 17). He disappeared and "a great silence followed." The inarticulate sensations of the crowd mirror those of Mr. Cumming after he had seen his wife fall into the river: "[they] may, in some measure, be conceived, but they cannot be described" (*P*, 15). There is no langauge to describe the assimilation of Patch and Mrs. Cumming into the Falls and the river below

> : a body found next spring
> frozen in an ice-cake; or a body
> fished next day from the muddy swirl—
> both silent, uncommunicative

If Patch and Mrs. Cumming now understand the unity of self and world, the dream and the reality, they cannot speak. And the great difficulty for Williams is that he feels his poem too verges on "the uncommunicative." Having made contact with the earth, the world of the sleeping giants which the "great beast" cannot understand, Williams has cut himself off from the people. "The theme" of his poem, he writes,

> is as it may prove: asleep, unrecognized—
> all of a piece, alone
> in a wind that does not move the others—
>
> (*P*, 19)

As opposed to the others, the "great beast," Williams is "all of a piece" with the land, as is the poem. But the poem is as asleep and unrecognized as the landscape of the sleeping giants whose bodies, lying together in love, define the land itself. And the poet who has created this harmony suddenly finds himself "alone"— an anomalous unity of one. The poet's aim is to rediscover a speech which would include the real, "the great beast," in its poetic saying. Williams sees "a kind of springtime/ toward which" the minds of his people aspire, but which, because he cannot communicate it, remains "within himself—ice bound" (*P*, 36).

Throughout the early books of *Paterson* the poet is "ice-bound" as he attempts to recover an original, unifying speech, some "music that is whole, unequivocal" (*P*, 60) which lies asleep beneath the myriad voices of the crowd on a "Sunday in the Park."[4] Book One ends by pointing toward the cavern of the Paterson Falls where "shut from/ the world—and unknown to the world" waits "shrounded there"

> Earth, the chatterer, father of all
> speech . . .
>
> (*P*, 39)

Williams the poet attempts to rend the veil in order to discover that origin and that ground where poetry and prose are one, "the language" which is "all speech." In his effort to synthesize, the implicit project of Williams's poem becomes the attempt to elevate the mere saying of the "great beast" to poetic saying. An earlier exchange between a poet, P., and an unknown voice demonstrates the danger that the poet runs when he thinks he can translate anew the roar of the Falls by ignoring the roar of the great beast:

> Into the sewer they threw the dead horse.
> What birth does this foretell? I think
> he'll write a novel bye and bye   .
>
> P. Your interest is in the bloody loam but what
>   I'm after is the finished product.
>   (P, 37)

In a sense P., in rejecting the "bloody loam," is rarefying it and thus is in danger of finding his poetic space "all of a piece, alone." P.'s reply to the unnamed voice affirms the primacy of poetry's "finished product" over "the bloody loam" which is the stuff of the novel. Williams, on the other hand, attempts to create a unity, an original ground for speech, by including the "bloody loam"—whether seen as prose, the roar of the great beast, or the artifacts of the beast's city—in the space of poetry, in the realm of "a mathematic calm, controlled, the architecture" (P, 38) of ordered verse:

> Plaster saints, glass jewels
> and those apt paper flowers, bafflingly
> complex—have here
> their forthright beauty, beside;
>
> Things, things unmentionable,
> the sink with the waste farina in it and
> lumps of rancid meat, milk-bottle-tops: have
> here a tranquility and loveliness
> Have here (in his thoughts)
> a complement tranquil and chaste.
>
>   He shifts his change:

"The 7th, December, this year, (1737) at night was a large shock
of an earthquake, accompanied with a remarkable rumbling noise;
people waked in their beds, the doors flew open, bricks fell from
the chimneys; the consternation was serious, but happily no great
damage ensued."

(*P*, 38–39)

Williams is aiming here for a synthesis of opposites, a unified,
homogeneous vision. Oddly enough, he ends up outlining instead one of the important functions of an aesthetics of heterogeneity, a willing (or at least inevitable) refusal to synthesize
opposites. The very material Williams attempts to ennoble by
including it in his poetry ends up simultaneously asserting itself
as itself. If, as Williams wrote to Moore, his attempt to create
unity in *Paterson* is "an essential failure," the poem itself begins
to delineate a new aesthetic position. Williams's attempt to create unity begins "here," where—by their presence in the poem—
both the waste of the city and the most tawdry of its products
("plaster saints, glass jewels") are metamorphosed and en-
nobled. When Williams says that "he shifts his change," he
means us to see his pun; that is, he shifts from one sort of junk
(saints and jewels, farina and milk-bottle-tops) which has been
metamorphosed by its inclusion in the poem to a second sort of
junk (prose fragments). The implication is that, discovering itself
"here" in the poem, the prose, like the plaster saints, has been
dignified with a "forthright beauty."[5] Williams sees here only
the creation of poetic unity, not the inherent and simultaneous
suggestion of its opposite.

Throughout Book One (and until Book Three, as a matter of
fact) Williams conceives of his project as distinctly ameliorative.
In the same way that he approaches the American idiom in the
"Detail" poems of the late 1930s, he approaches the prose of
Paterson as unformed verse; his project is to form it. The poem
remains for him, as he says near the end of Book Two, "the
most perfect rock and temple" (*P*, 80), and for the "thrashing,
breeding/ . debased city" (*P*, 81) to be raised to its elevation
remains his dream. Williams implicitly compares his poem, in
fact, to an old Aztec sculpture of a red basalt grasshopper, the
concrete weight of which finds "a counter buoyancy" in the
"mind's wings" (*P*, 48):

—his mind a red stone carved to be
endless flight   .
Love that is a stone endlessly in flight,
so long as stone shall last bearing
the chisel's stroke   .

(*P*, 49)

The order which the mind imposes on the world, the peaceable union of opposites which "love" implies, the relative permanence and stability of art as opposed to the transience and fragility of the flesh—all of these are what Williams sees as the poem's promise to its concrete subject matter. "The stone lives, the flesh dies" (*P*, 49), he reminds us. To be elevated into the world of art is to be saved.

But two forces in Book Two work against this quasi-spiritual poetry of affirmation. In the first place, his most ambitious attempt to remake prose into poetry fails by his own admission. He reacts to Klaus Ehrens's sermon, which occupies the better part of eight pages, by concluding that it hangs "featureless/ upon the ear" (*P*, 70). He not only must ask himself "Is this the only beauty here?" but also, more honestly, "is this beauty" (*P*, 71)? Second, the Marcia Nardi letters possess a power which allows the prose to assert itself as a major force in the poem for the first time. Almost every occurrence of prose in Book One details an instance of deformity and occurs in the midst of the poem's own discussion of deformity. There the prose is used in the manner of *example*. It contributes, in fact, to the poetry of deformity to which Book One's concluding quotation from Symonds's *Studies of the Greek Poets* subscribes—a poetry which displays an "acute aesthetic sense of propriety, recognizing the harmony which subsists between crabbed verses and the disturbed subjects with which they dealt. . . . Deformed verse was suited to deformed morality" (*P*, 40). Prose is, for Williams, the most "deformed verse" of all. The Nardi letters also serve Book Two by way of example. Their subject is the divorce of male from female and of man from his fellow man. But the Nardi letters do more than serve as examples of divorce and its consequences; they also challenge the ameliorative pull of Williams's art, his vision of marriage and his sense that art can elevate its world. For instance, Williams is willing to interrupt his nearly rhapsodic tribute to the Aztec grasshopper with an excerpt from one of the letters. Its presence at this moment in the poem, with Nardi's accusation that by ignoring her letters Williams has destroyed "the validity for me myself *of* myself" (*P,* 48), challenges the conviction of the lines about the Aztec sculpture. How is it that Williams's mind is a stone in "endless flight," that "Love" is this same stone, and yet Williams can act so lovelessly? The last letter, which concludes Book Two in six and a half very long pages, functions in much the same way, but even more powerfully suggests the pull of prose toward the world in which it originated. The poetry ends with Williams regaining

> the sun kissed summits of love!
>
>   .   .   .   .
>
> —saying over to himself a song written
> previously .   inclines to believe
> he sees, in the structure, something
>   of interest:
>
> On this most voluptuous night of the year
> the term of the moon is yellow with no light
> the air's soft, the night bird has
> only one note, the cherry tree in bloom
>
>   .   .   .   .
>
>   Now love might enjoy its play
> and nothing disturb the full octave of its run
>   (*P,* 85–86)

I have not quoted the concluding "song" in its entirety here, but it consists of three quatrains (of which I include the first four and last two lines). It is, in short, as lyrical, as tranquil, as controlled, and as *visually* ordered (Williams *sees* in the structure something of interest) a moment as has occurred in *Paterson* up to this point. It projects the marriage of opposites toward which Williams has been working. And yet this unity is undercut by its artificiality, its withdrawal into the world of art. The poet "says over," almost as an incantation, "a song written/ previously," a song which would assert unity by keeping chaos, heterogeneity, at bay. It is a "song" and a "structure" which the poet "inclines to believe": it is a dream of unity, not unity itself. The Nardi letter denies Williams his lyric victory. It accuses him of being one of a number of American writers who are "sheltered from life in the raw by the glass-walled conditions of their own safe lives" (P, 87), of abandoning love and friendship, of precipitating anger, indignation, and loneliness, and finally of abdicating any concern for what is *real* in life. The Nardi letter calls into question—and it does have the last word—the whole direction of Williams's effort up to this point in the poem. It charges that Williams's ameliorative verse has abandoned life for "art," that he has rarefied the poem into a world of art which has nothing to do with the world itself.

This would be a just enough accusation were it not for the presence in the poem of the letter itself. The letter brings the poem back into the world. As I have indicated, largely because of the letter's presence Book Two was less than enthusiastically received, and Williams defended its inclusion at least twice in 1948, in letters to Parker Tyler and Horace Gregory. "It *is*," he wrote to Tyler, "that prose and verse are both *writing*, both a matter of the words. . . . I want to say that prose and verse are to me the same thing, that verse . . . belongs *with* prose. . . . [Poetry] goes *along with* prose and, companionably, by itself, without aid or excuse or need for separation or bolstering, shows itself by *itself* for what it is. *It belongs* there, in the gutter" (*SL*, 263). To Gregory he wrote virtually the same thing: "The truth is that there's an *identity* between prose and verse, not an antithesis. . . . But, specifically, as you see, the long letter is definitely germane to the rest of the text. . . . That it is *not* the same stuff as the poem but comes from below 14th St. is precisely the key" (*SL*, 265). If these defenses seem to contradict themselves, it is because Williams—working on Books Three and Four when he wrote to Tyler and Gregory—had begun to understand that his work was leading toward an aesthetic of heterogeneity. He had, despite himself, been trying to bring the poem to a homogeneous conclusion, to a vision of synthesis and marriage. Poetry and prose were to be part of this unity, and even in his letters to Tyler and Gregory he is perhaps still suggesting that there is one ground—"Earth," which is the origin, "father of all/ speech." Yet as he continually fails to uncover this "shrouded," unifying origin, he discovers instead that the prose in *Paterson* functions in two ways simultaneously. On the one hand, because the prose is a part of the poem *Paterson,* it is poetry; prose and poetry are an "identity." On the other hand, because it "comes from below 14th St.," prose is differentiated from poetry. Poetry shows "itself by *itself* for what it is," and so does prose. To paraphrase Williams's own oxymoron, they go together, companionably, by themselves. The prose, in fact, functions very much like Duchamp's urinal: the urinal in the museum and a urinal below 14th St. in a plumber's shop are simultaneously identical and not. They share the fact that they are composed of the same material; they differ in the nature of the space they occupy and define. It is the implicit juxtaposition of these two urinals (the same and not the same) that makes for the ready-made's vitality as art. And it is the explicit juxtaposition of prose and poetry (likewise the same and not the same) that generates Williams's poem.

The Nardi letters, furthermore, call into question Williams's authority as poet. He is not, after all, the "author" of these texts included in his poem; instead, he is the person to whom the texts are directed. In a discussion of the function of the extra-authorial text in poetry, Jacques Ehrmann has put the matter very clearly:

> One can no longer say that the poet is at the *origin* of his language, since it is language which creates the poet and not the reverse. . . . "I" is therefore in the "texts," but not as subject at their origin—that is to say, not as their "author"—but as their object, the one who must be sought precisely because he is absent from them. . . . In this manner the "text" loses the sacred character which in our culture we have been pleased to confer upon it. Sacred (poetic) language and ordinary language cease to oppose one another like an aristocrat and a plebian. . . . We no longer confront poetry as though we were standing at the threshold of a church, a place that evokes all that is "sacred" to the profane, that immediately triggers the response: attention, sanctuary!, or its literary equivalent: attention, poetry!, automatically engendering an attitude of constrained respect and stiff decorum in

marked contrast to the coarsest profanations and irregularities of
everyday life and language. . . . To write would now be first of
all to quote. The "writer" would not be the one who "listens to
a voice from within," but rather the one who quotes, who puts
language in quotes.[6]

The effect of the Nardi letters on *Paterson* is to challenge the
authority of Williams's art in exactly the way Ehrmann's suggestive discussion outlines. They reverse the ameliorative strain of
the poem and expose it as "aristocratic" (exactly Nardi's point
when she argues that Williams is "sheltered from life"). Williams
is surely conscious of this: he is willing not only to place the
letters where he does, but also to admit to Tyler that poetry
belongs with prose, "in the gutter." For the first time the poem
clearly attains the ambiguity which marks an aesthetics of heterogeneity—a simultaneity, not a synthesis, of opposites. The
poem promises us unity in its preface:

> it can't be
> otherwise—an
> interpenetration, both ways. Rolling
> up! Obverse, reverse;
> the drunk the sober; the illustrious
> the gross; one.
> (*P*, 3–4)

During the poem, however, the dream of unity ("one") is challenged by its heterogeneous material ("both ways"). And Williams's loss of authority—his authorial "absence," so to speak—
brings the poem down from its "Sacred rock and temple" and
into contact with the profane which initiates the "interpenetration" he promises. The poet himself, in fact, becomes part of
the ambiguity of his poem: the force of his persona Paterson—
itself ambiguous as both poet and city—is to make the poet, as
the letters do, both subject and object in his own poem; the
name itself, Pater/son, suggests both father and son, both creator
and created.

Ehrmann also clarifies the nature of Williams's collage. It is
an assemblage of quotations: "He hears! Voices . indeterminate!" (*P*, 45).[7] Book Two ended with the juxtaposition of his

extended quotation from Nardi and his quotation from himself ("Saying over to himself a song written/ previously"). Within the text the authors Nardi and Williams are accorded equal status; outside the text the author Williams assembles his materials, a letter and a poem. The power of the Nardi letter, however, throws into question the idea of poetic authority; Williams's own project is undermined by Nardi's authorial view. Book Three, which opens with an epigraph from Santayana, continues the juxtaposition of quotation which closed Book Two (if we can call that sort of ambiguity "closure"). Settled in the library—the repository and reliquary of written language— Williams assembles a collage of quotations and paraphrased fragments: from a history—"The last wolf was killed near the Weisse Huis in the year 1723" (*P*, 97); from a personal letter written by an unknown author—"Hell, New Jersey," (*P*, 97); from old newspaper files, various paraphrases—"a child burned in a field . . . The Paterson Cricket Club, 1896. A woman lobbyist . . . Two local millionaires—moved away . . . another Indian rock shelter found—a bone awl . . . the old Rogers Locomotive Works" (*P*, 98);[8] from his own story—the "Gently! Gently!" stanza of his 1937 "Paterson: Episode 17" (*CEP*, 439; *P*, 98); from anecdote, as we hear the fictional voice of Lambert, mill owner, who opposed unions—

> This is MY shop I reserve the right (and he did)
> to walk down the row (between his looms) and
> fire any son-of-a-bitch I choose without excuse
> or reason more than that I don't like his face.
>
> (*P*, 99)

What becomes clear when we look at this assemblage of material is that Williams the poet does not have—or, at least, will not exercise—the same authority as Lambert the industrialist. The poet cannot say of the world "this is MY shop" and be rid of what he doesn't like. Williams cannot choose to "fire any son-of-a-bitch I choose without excuse" because, as he said in "To All Gentleness,"

> they speak,
> euphemistically, of the anti-poetic!
> Garbage. Half the world ignored . . .
>
> (*CLP*, 24)

As the inclusion of his own poem in the assemblage of quotation demonstrates, Williams can no longer claim special authority even over his own earlier work. But Williams as author does assert himself by controlling the form of the material within the space of the poem. All these quotations are held together by the repeated phrase "So be it," which at one time points to the inability of the poet to change or ignore the material which makes up his shop and his concomitant ability to arrange this material. That the poem *Paterson* will become an object in the world like any other object is foreseen by the inclusion of his "Gently! Gently!" stanza in this assemblage. Poetry and the special vatic status of the poet have been desanctified, but the poet remains the artificer.

Paterson denies the possibility of ever realizing the dreams of synthesis with which it had begun, but it does not deny the reality of the dream itself. The dream is in fact a crucial term in the collision of values, the heterogeneity, of which the poem is made. In "The Neglected Artist" Williams writes: "May it not be that the world of art does offer an asylum, a working place for the reestablishment of order? There must be order, there must be discipline—without destruction of the variables which often hold the new direction among them" (*RI*, 91). This reestablishment of order occupies Williams through most of Book Three, but he is careful to point out that he will not leave the "library stench"—the prosaic coarseness of reality—behind. He will follow the example of Toulouse-Lautrec, who, deformed himself and living among the whores, "recorded them" and made art of them (*P*, 110). He will "Embrace the/ foulness" (*P*, 103). He will be as "recreant" as fire, but like the fire he is re-creative (*P*, 117):

> An old bottle, mauled by the fire
> gets a new glaze, the glass warped
> to a new distinction, reclaiming the
> undefined. A hot stone, reached
> by the tide, crackled over by fine
> lines, the glaze unspoiled .
> Annihilation ameliorated
>
> .   .   .   .

—the flame that wrapped the glass
deflowered, reflowered there by
the flame: a second flame, surpassing
heat .

. . . . .

Poet Beats Fire at Its Own Game! The bottle!
the bottle! the bottle! the bottle! I
give you the bottle! What's burning
now, Fire?
　　　　　　(*P*, 118)

"What's burning now" is the flame of creation which surpasses the fire's flame. The old bottle here is perhaps the same old bottle that Williams re-created from the ashes in the poem "Between Walls." (He had explicated the poem in a letter to Babette Deutsch as Book Three was getting under way.[9]) Both bottle poems suggest the image of the phoenix; both are re-created out of their own destruction.

In short, *Paterson* embodies a double movement. It is both destructive and ameliorative—and it cannot be one without first having been the other. Nevertheless, Williams finds himself still "Seeking," which is the concluding remark of the first part of Book Three (*P*, 112). What he seeks, again, is a unity which denies the simultaneity of his own poem: "*a* speech—is, of necessity, my sole concern," he says near the end of Book Three (*P*, 144). What he seeks is a single speech out of "the roar of the present" (*P*, 144), which is both the "uproar of water falling" and the "roar" of the "great beast," the two languages confronting him. And his own poetry represents a third voice which attempts to speak "the Language" of Earth and remains unheard in the din. "Who am I?" he asks. Instead of a direct reply, he exclaims:

　　　　　　　　　　—the voice!
　　　　　—the voice rises, neglected
　　　(with its new) the unfaltering
　　　language.
　　　　　　(*P*, 107–8)

He is the neglected artist who attempts in faltering verse to recapture "*the* voice" of Earth, "*the* unfaltering language." As a result of his failure to speak "all speech" and to be heard, he tells himself to give up poetry, "Give up the shilly/ shally of art" (*P,* 108). For him, "the words are lacking" (*P,* 120); he knows nothing out of which he can form a speech that will suffice. He wants to know "how to begin to find a shape" for the poem, a proposition which "seems beyond attainment" (*P,* 140), because this single shape must be capable of accommodating *"this,* this/ this, this, this, this" (*P,* 141), a plurality of things.

What Williams is after at the end of Book Three is the variable foot, the stanzaic pattern which is at once a single shape and capable of accommodating a multiplicity of things, even the multiple rhythms of the American idiom. It does not find its way into *Paterson* until Book Five's appearance. Book Four, originally thought of as the poem's conclusion, is still troubled by its inability simultaneously to be both plural and unified, concrete and abstract. The book admits that it "fails mastery." What the poet desires is

> To bring himself in,
> hold together wives in one wife and
> at the same time scatter it,
> the one in all of them   .
>   Weakness,
> weakness dogs him, fulfillment only
> a dream or in a dream.
>   (*P,* 191)

This dream is the same as the one with which *Paterson* began— a dream of marriage and homogeneity juxtaposed to a world of divorce and heterogeneity. Throughout Book Four (throughout *Paterson,* but not as consciously) Williams is fighting this dream of wholeness and unity. This first section of Book Four, for instance, images modern love in terms derived not from the ideals of fulfillment but from the aesthetics of the machine. The unsuccessful "marriage" between the sophisticated lesbian Corydon and the country-maid Phyllis is an open parody of the pastoral. Here love is mechanized and sexless:

> in the tall
> buildings (sliding up and down) . . . where

```
              the money's made
                    up and down
                          directed missles
        in the greased shafts of the tall buildings   .
                  .      .      .      .

                          unsexed, up
        and down (without wing motion)
                                    (P, 165)
```

To be without "wing motion" is to be without imagination, without even the possibility of creative ordering. There is no wholeness in this modern instance.

The second section links Madame Curie's discovery of radium to "a plan for action" which would eliminate "money." Curie's discovery of radium resulted, Williams writes, from her realization that there is a "dissonance/ in the valence of uranium":

```
        Dissonance
        (if you are interested)
        leads to discovery
                          (P, 176)
```

Her discovery is a metaphor for the discovery Williams himself has been seeking throughout the poem, and her method, he realizes, is his own: "Love, the sledge that smashes the atom? No, No! antagonistic cooperation is the key" (P, 177). This is an explicit denial of the dream of unity or, more precisely, of the dream that life is itself the realization of unity. Dissonance, or antagonistic cooperation of opposites, is what makes the new element, just as the dissonance between abstraction and reality is what makes Williams's new poem. This dissonance, he claims, has been mirrored throughout the poem, especially in its juxtaposition of poetry and prose, a juxtaposition as old as Chaucer and springing from the necessity for difference, for different ways of saying:

```
Sir Thopas (The Canterbury Pilgrims) says (to Chaucer)
        Namoor—
        Thy drasty rymyng is not
        worth a toord
—and Chaucer seemed to think so too for he stopped and went
on in prose   .   [10]
        (P, 177)
```

But Curie's achievement lies in her ability to break down her world into its constituent parts, to separate the radium's "radiant gist" (*P*, 186) from the dead weight which carries it. This also is the value of August Walter's "credit" scheme: credit, Williams claims, is "stalled/ in money" (*P*, 183), it is the "radiant gist" of financial dealings and can be separated from "money." So, too, poetry is the "radiant gist" of all language. Curie's discovery of radium—a "LUMINOUS" discovery that Williams compares to the discovery of America by quoting his own *In the American Grain* (*P*, 178; *IAG*, 25–26)—verifies Mendeleev's projection of the existence of radium in his standard table of molecular weights. Paterson's own projection—that a poetry can be discovered which will accommodate all manner of juxtaposition—is pure thought, like Mendeleev's table, a poem which charts the path for subsequent discoveries:

> adept at thought, playing the words
> following a table which is the synthesis
> of thought, a symbol that is to him [Paterson],
> sun up! a Mendelief, the elements laid
> out by molecular weight, identity
> predicted before found! and   .
> Oh most powerful connective, a bead
> to lie between continents through
> which a string passes   .
>
> (*P*, 179)

This pure thought, the possibility that the "radiant gist" of language might be found now that Williams has predicted it, connects the continents of abstraction and reality.

This Mendeleev passage is one of the most crucial in all of Williams's poetry, for it significantly modifies his dialectic between mind and matter. The opposition between abstraction and reality in fact remains, but the mind now rests between the two: "the mind is neutral, a bead linking/ continents, brow and toe" (*P*, 179). The opposition between the abstract and the real is embodied in the image of man himself. The *active* mind, its "playing," is now the "most powerful connective," a paradigm for antagonistic cooperation, the dissonance between the split forces of the world, inevitably "playing" with them all. Furthermore, the passage almost guarantees the continuation of Williams's struggle to realize a speech adequate to the plurality of his vision. The next generation of poets, Allen Ginsberg's letter testifies, will attempt to discover it: "I envision for myself some kind of new speech . . . in that it has to be clear statement of fact about misery (and not misery itself), and splendor . . . out of the subjective wanderings through Paterson. . . . I know you will be pleased to realize that at least one actual citizen of your community has inherited your experience in his struggle to love and know his own world-city" (*P*, 174). "*La Vertue*," Williams writes, "*est toute dans l'effort*" (*P*, 189). In other words, the point of *Paterson* has turned out to be not the realization of any dream, but the effort itself, the making and the project it defines.

In *The Inverted Bell* Joseph Riddel has pointed out that if Book Four "has received the most consistent critical disapprobation," seeming "to critics to be the most absurdly disrelated" of *Paterson*'s five parts, that is because of its daring exploration of "the freedom of language, of past languages, to change."[11] The changes, it should be quickly noted, are not always for the better. As Corydon's poetry is to the pastoral tradition, and

> As Carrie Nation
>   to Artemis
>   so is our life today
>   (*P*, 180)

And so too is our language. The risk that Williams is beginning to assume by Book Four is the danger of opening his art to his sons (to the son he takes to hear the lecture on atomic fission, and to his poetic sons such as Ginsberg), of risking his art's abuse. That is, Curie's discovery of radium has led not only to extraordinary scientific possibilities but also to the bomb. And the bomb to Williams is the ultimate expression of "the great beast," of those who "are used to death and/ jubilate at it" (*P*, 200).

Thus the dissonance of Book Four, the disrelated nature of its three parts, is at once the expression of the multiplicity and degradation of the age itself (a structural image of the same dissonance that exists between the three "lovers"—Paterson,

Phyllis, and Corydon—in the first part) and the projection of an as yet unrealized poetic potential to be born of the poem's very dissonance. To put it another way, there are two competing versions of human interaction in Book Four. The first is epitomized by the dialogues between Corydon and Phyllis, Phyllis and Paterson: empty exchanges characterized by dissimulation, evasion, and interiorization. The second is epitomized by the letters from Ginsberg: revelatory, open, and frank, they initiate a dialogue about the nature of the poem that remains open ended and ongoing. One is static, dead even; the other is vital, just as for Corydon the landscape is "docile" (*P*, 152), while for Ginsberg it is "alive and busy" (*P*, 194).

Williams's rather obvious preference for Ginsberg's point of view begins to explain his rejection at the end of Book Four of his inaugural plan, the final assimilation of the poet into the sea, with all the overt symbolic weight of unification, totalization, and completion that the run to the sea carries with it. To end the drift of the poem, to formally close it, would be to end the dialogue he is just commencing with his sons. It would be to deny the heterogeneity—thematic, structural, and interpretative—to which he has opened the poem itself. Riddel notes that "*Paterson*, therefore, is necessarily a pre-text; just as the books in the Library are the pretexts of *Paterson*. . . . The poem ends in a reversal . . . which opens the poem to continuation by other sons,"[12] and to continuation even by Williams himself, he who is simultaneously father and son, Pater/son. Thus, even as a voice exhorts Williams to "Come on, get going. The tide's in" (*P*, 188), Williams begins to chatter again and returns not to the sea but to the historical texts and fragments of the First Book: "perhaps/ it is not too late?" he wonders (*P*, 187).

Reports of murder and death are scattered throughout the last section so that Williams might reject them:

> You come today to see killed
> killed, killed
> as if it were a conclusion
> —a conclusion!
> a convincing strewing of corpses
> —to move the mind
> as tho' the mind

can be moved, the mind, I said
by an array of hacked corpses
(*P*, 199)

Death and conclusion do not move us; life and beginnings do. We are at the moment that the poem's cryptic epigraph announced, the moment where a new "plan for action" supplants the original (*P*, 2). We are about to witness the "dispersal" and "metamorphosis" (*P*, 2) of art which is the subject of Book Five.

NOTES

1. The notion of an "aesthetic of heterogeneity" is Lawrence Alloway's. He uses it in connection with Robert Rauschenberg's combine-paintings in his introductory essay to the catalogue for the large Rauschenberg retrospective which toured the country from October 1976 to January 1978 (*Robert Rauschenberg* [Washington: Smithsonian Institution, National Collection of Fine Arts, 1976], p. 5). J. Hillis Miller has also argued for the essential heterogeneity of *Paterson* in "Deconstructing the Deconstructers," a review of Joseph Riddel's *The Inverted Bell: Modernism and the Counter Poetics of William Carlos Williams* (Baton Rouge: Louisiana State University Press, 1974), in *Diacritics* 5 (Summer 1975): 24–31.

2. Sergei Eisenstein, *Film Form*, ed. and trans. Jay Leyda (New York: Harcourt Brace & World, 1949), p. 38. In the opening "Walking" sequence of *Paterson*, Book Two, itself quite clearly a conscious example of montage, Williams refers specifically to Eisenstein (*P*, 58).

3. Randall Jarrell, *Poetry and the Age* (New York: Knopf, 1953), p. 262. For other similar reactions see also Paul L. Mariani, *William Carlos Williams: The Poet and His Critics* (Chicago: American Library Association, 1975), pp. 83–89.

4. The importance of the idea of recovering "origin" in Williams's work and in *Paterson* particularly is, of course, not original with me. It is the organizing principle of Riddel's *Inverted Bell*. I agree with Riddel that Williams's eventual success rests in his willingness to give up the necessity for the poet to recover an original, holistic speech. I am not so willing to agree that Williams instead repeatedly rediscovers "the original moment as original violation" (p. 298). That is, I am not quite sure how one gives up seeking "the original moment" and yet repeatedly rediscovers it, although if Riddel means by "original violation" what he calls "the imaginative play that is and always has been at the center of history . . . the freedom to interpret" (pp. 297–98), then, as my last chapter will suggest, perhaps our sense of Williams's achievement is very close indeed.

5. In the Yale MS for the "Notes and Early Drafts" for Book One, Williams explains that the glass jewels at least possess a "forthright beauty" because "they are valued by an order." The order to which he refers must be the order of the poem itself.

6. Jacques Ehrmann, "The Death of Literature," *New Literary History* 3 (Autumn 1971): 34–37.

7. As an assembler of quotations Williams is what Lévi-Strauss calls, in *The Savage Mind* (Chicago: University of Chicago Press, 1966), a *bricoleur*. Williams lifts his heterogeneous quotations into the poem, appropriates them to his own purpose, and makes them function in a new way. Powell Woods, in "William Carlos Williams: The Poet as Engineer," *Profile of William Carlos Williams*, ed. Jerome Mazzaro (Columbus: Charles E. Merrill, 1971), pp. 79–90, seeks to prove that Williams is the opposite of the *bricoleur*, the engineer who attempts to employ new techniques and a new vocabulary to serve his formal designs. Woods dismisses the role of *bricolage* in Williams's work because he assumes that the "residue of human artifacts" which is the *bricoleur*'s material is, by definition, "tradition-conscious and derivative" (p. 82). This is simply not true. The *bricoleur* effects a discontinuity with tradition when he makes a new thing of the old material. Woods seems to be assuming that to be a *bricoleur* is to be somehow conservative and uninventive. That is like saying that Williams is conservative and uninventive when he puts a letter from Nardi into his poem. Worse, Woods seems to have missed one of the major points of *The Savage Mind:* that "primitive" myth-making, in which *bricolage* dominates, is not the half-baked forerunner of modern science, but a different, parallel, and equally admirable order of thought. Lévi-Strauss is careful to point out, furthermore, that most artists are equally *bricoleurs* and engineers. This is a much more reasonable way to approach Williams's work.

8. All of this material is drawn from articles in *The Prospector: Weekly Newspaper for Northern New Jersey Devoted to Historical Interests* for 1936, as Benjamin Sankey points out in *A Companion to Paterson* (Berkeley: University of California Press, 1971), p. 123. Sankey's book has been very useful to me, especially in its discussion of the poem's prose. The detailed discussions provided by Sankey's book, Riddel's, Joel Conarroe's *Paterson: Language and Landscape* (Philadelphia: University of Pennsylvania Press, 1970), and Walter Scott Peterson's *An Approach to Paterson* (New Haven: Yale University Press, 1967) in fact free me to approach the poem from a more general point of view. Rather than summarizing the poem, or even explicating it, I hope it is clear that I am only outlining the drift of a developing aesthetic, explaining why the poem takes the shape it does.

9. *Selected Letters*, pp. 264–65. Thirlwall identifies the "green bottle piece" to which Williams refers in the letter as "On the Road to the

Contagious Hospital" (note 264). He cannot be right; there is no bottle in "*By* the Road. . . ."

10. In his letter to Parker Tyler justifying the Nardi letter in *Paterson*, Williams quotes this same passage from Chaucer (*SL*, 263).

11. Riddel, *The Inverted Bell*, p. 237.

12. Ibid., p. 247.

CHAPTER FIVE

The Visual Text

In the October 1952 number of *Poetry* Williams announced his intention to continue with the poem he had supposedly completed the year before by publishing a version of the first lines of what would later become "Asphodel, That Greeny Flower" under the title of *"Paterson,* Book Five: The River of Heaven."[1] The subtitle survives nowhere else in his finished work, though it had a long life in manuscript.[2] It refers to the Milky Way, and in the context of *Paterson* as a whole it shifts the locus of the poem from the banks of the Passaic to more ethereal reaches. Asked to define poetry by the St. John's College literary magazine early that same year, Williams had written: "Poetry along with the other arts represents a man's longing to make one with his fellows through the ages upon a basis which asserts their mutual love for the eternal and divine" (Yale MS). By explicitly aligning itself with art and artists "through the ages," the projected fifth book of *Paterson* would apparently move into this realm of the eternal and divine. But a few years earlier Williams had also written, toward the end of his *Autobiography,* that in *Paterson* he wanted "to write about the people close to me: to know in detail, minutely what I was talking about—to the whites of their eyes, to their very smells" (*A,* 391). The two points of view can be reconciled—"the local is the universal," he would often say—but the difference in emphasis from the first four books to the projected fifth is a marked one. Considering his unwillingness, at the end of Book Four, to enter the sea, that "nostalgic/ mother" in whom the dead are "enwombed," his

desire to immerse himself in some "river of heaven" in Book
Five seems almost an act of self-betrayal.

More particularly, Williams suddenly seems to want to leave
the world behind, "to take the world of Paterson into a new
dimension," as he wrote his publisher (*P*, "Author's Note"). The
project is to regain the wholeness of heaven:

> It is a measure
> > set to the dance
> > > as the ancients knew
> —which we have lost
> > and may regain again
> > > there is a Paradisio
>
> > > > ("The River of Heaven," Yale MS)

He praises all poems—specifically those of Homer and Dante—
which led us "to a view . . . of heaven" (Yale MS). The "river
of heaven," he says, is a "timeless sea"—clearly the same sea he
had rejected in Book Four:

> If you would be remembered
> > to the rose
> > > add the timelessness
> of the sea
> > and you have the rhythm:
> > > a rose , is a rose ,
> is a rose , is a rose
> > in perpetuity
> > > It is the river
> of heaven
> > which in the end
> > > absorbs all our lives.
>
> > > > ("The River of Heaven," Yale MS)

What he envisioned, finally, for the new fifth book of *Paterson*
was the perfect revelation of a new measure in the poem, the
elevation of the world into the perfection of heaven. "No prose,"
he admonished himself. "Uniform throughout in form to embody whatever I have learned of form (with variants): a triple
line (all the same line really) on three levels across the page.
Unchanging" (Yale MS).

The poem that turned out to be his image for the all-absorbing wholeness of heaven, "uniform throughout in form," was, of course, "Asphodel." But, while "Asphodel" remains "a celebration of the light" (to borrow his own phrase), it claims, significantly, much less for itself than it had in its initial stages, when it had sought to reveal "the river of heaven." It finally takes its title, after all, not from the Milky Way but from some odorless flower said to grace the shores of hell. Part of this revision may be attributed to Williams's reacquaintance, as he decided on what to include in the *Selected Essays* (1959), with an essay he had written in 1939. In "Against the Weather: A Study of the Artist," he had attacked the conception of Dante's *Paradiso:*

> Both the *Commedia* and the *Libro de Buen Amor* have love as their theme, earthly and heavenly. But earthly love, in its own right (Paolo and Francesca) is condemned in the *Commedia* and celebrated to the full in the *Book—free* to the winds.
>
> .   .   .   .
>
> There is likely to prove as time passes more good in the *Book of Love* than could ever be contained in Dante's *Paradiso.* That is why the *Paradiso* is so much weaker than the *Inferno.* (*SE*, 204–5)

His "celebration of the light"—which is, after all, a celebration of his love for Flossie, not for some Beatrice—is a poem in the "earthly" tradition. Moreover, what Williams praises about Dante's poetic line is *not* its "uniformity throughout" but its "fault," its "celebration of denial":

> The dogmatist in Dante chose a triple multiple for his poem, the craftsman skilfully followed orders—but the artist?
>   Note that beginning with the first line of the *terza rima* at any given onset, every four lines following contain a dissonance. . . . Throughout the *Commedia* this fourth unrhymed factor, unobserved . . . restores it to the candid embrace of love. (*SE*, 207)

"Asphodel" is indeed virtually uniform throughout and may well embody all that Williams had learned of his new line. But if he once planned this same uniformity of line for *Paterson*, Book Five, he rejected it in favor of a more dissonant structure—in favor, once again, of a collage of verse and prose-letters from

Edward Dahlberg, Ezra Pound, and Allen Ginsberg, sketches
by Mezz Mezzrow and Gilbert Sorrentino, and an interview
with Mike Wallace. The prose in Book Five is no longer representative of some inarticulate speech which must be elevated to
poetry, but is instead a necessary dissonance, part and parcel of
the poem itself.

This is not to say, of course, that the attractions of "heaven"
are not also part and parcel of the poem, equally necessary to
its dissonance. Book Five, which finally appeared in 1958, begins in fact by literally leaving the world behind:

>   In old age
>   the mind
>   casts off
>   rebelliously
>   an eagle
>   from its crag
>   (*P*, 207)

But a moment later it returns to "the rock/ the bare rocks" (*P*,
207), to a consideration of "the thing itself" (*P*, 208). Book Five,
as a whole, weaves back and forth between heaven and earth,
mind and matter, in precisely this way, not so much balancing
its oppositions as allowing each its separate voice. Furthermore,
this opening passage draws as much attention to the materiality
of its words as to the transcendental and idealistic implications
of their reference. The lines are meant, first of all, to be *seen*.
Williams told Stanley Koehler in 1962 that he was "imitating
the flight of the bird" here, that the lines were meant to be taken
as a set of wings and were directed "to the eyes."[3]

In other words, a highly developed sensitivity to the poem's
material substance, its status as an object in the world, creates
a dissonance which competes with its more transcendental as-
pirations. It can be said, in fact, that the argument of Book Five
is with Williams's rebellious and airborne imagination. His recognition of the materiality of art—not only the materiality of
his own poem, but that of the unicorn tapestries at the Cloisters,
Brueghel's *Adoration of the Magi*, the paintings of Toulouse-

Lautrec, Paul Klee, Dürer, Bosch, Picasso, and Gris—represents for Williams a new, secular version of the fortunate fall. The drift of the imagination, its dream, is always toward the eternal and divine. But if the imagination is to survive, if it is to escape death "intact," it must quit its flight, fall through the "hole/ in the bottom of the bag," and descend into the material reality of its art (*P*, 212). The imagination, in fact, returns to the crag from which it cast off, makes contact with the rock, *through* art:

> Paterson, from the air
> > above the low range of its hills
> > > across the river
> on a rock-ridge
> > has returned to the old scenes
>
> .   .   .   .
>
> A WORLD OF ART
> THAT THROUGH THE YEARS HAS
>
> > > *SURVIVED!*
>
> —the museum became real
> > *The Cloisters*—
> > > on its rock
> casting its shadow—
> > > "la réalité! la réalité!
> > > > la réa, la réa, la réalité!"
> > > > > > (*P*, 209)[4]

The ethereal and disembodied unicorn is "faceless among the stars," an immaterial figure of the imagination "calling/ for its own murder" (*P*, 208) so that it might escape downward into art and be embodied in the final Cloisters tapestry as a beast held forever captive—"a collar round his neck" (*P*, 212)—a figure for the imagination now materialized in the garden of the world which is the tapestry itself. Similarly, "the beloved and sacred image" of the virgin (*P*, 234) must be whored, her purity brought down so that life—creation—might spring from her. The genius of Brueghel's great paintings rests in their representation of eternal and divine stories, such as the *Adoration,* in the most mundane terms:

> —it is a scene, authentic
> enough, to be witnessed frequently
> among the poor (I salute
> the man Brueghel who painted
> what he saw—
>
> (*P,* 226)

In short, in saluting art and the artistic imagination, Book Five salutes the material world, *what there is to see.*

II

There are, as I have said, two different things to see in Williams's late work—the visual *form* of his poetry, and the visual *art* which is the poetry's subject matter. By dedicating the fifth book of *Paterson* to Toulouse-Lautrec, by saluting the plastic arts generally, Williams draws attention to the importance of the visual to his idea of art. He turns, for instance, to the story of the immaculate conception in Book Five not only because of its thematic ties to the virgin-and-whore motif and its symbolic connection to the unicorn myth, but because it is the story of the necessity of the abstract and the ethereal to make itself concrete and actual. Only in the physical realm—in the actual embodiment of Christ—can "the eternal and divine" make itself known.

While the visual form of Book Five is varied and complex, partaking of the same heterogeneity which marks the first four books, I think it is fair to say that in almost every instance where Williams takes up the idea of the visual in general, and visual art in particular, he moves formally toward the staggered tercet.[5] At the bottom of the fifth book's first page, for instance, as the poem returns to the rock and consideration of "the thing itself," we encounter these lines:

> —it is a cloudy morning.
> He looks out the window
> sees the birds still there—
>
> (*P,* 207)

This is the first of four tercets preceding a prose intrusion. The intention, I think, is to draw the poem to *order* in the act of *looking*, to tie the idea of order to the visual realm.

It is important to differentiate the kind of visual order Williams achieves by means of the staggered tercet from the visual form of the lines imitating an eagle in flight which open the poem. The coherence of form and content presupposed by emblematic devices such as the eagle's wings simply goes against the grain of Williams's art, which is founded, after all, on the supposition that the imagination's ordering capabilities and the unruliness of the world exist simultaneously but not harmoniously. A dissonance always exists between the realms of the abstract and the real, between the form the poem takes and its subject matter. This is why J. Hillis Miller is wrong when he says that "a poem like 'The Yellow Chimney' is a picture of what it represents, the slender column of words corresponding to the chimney, and the lines of the poem, it may not be too fanciful to say, echoing the silver rings which strap the yellow stack at intervals."[6] The spatial design of "The Yellow Chimney" (*CLP,* 50) is in fact identical with that of a score of poems in *Pictures from Brueghel,* and it is as ridiculous to say that "Landscape with the Fall of Icarus" looks like a chimney as it is to suggest that the four stanzas which make up "The Red Wheelbarrow" look like little wheelbarrows.

If Williams's visual text amounted to no more than such a "picturing" of his subject matter, then Montaigne's classic indictment of such poetic "figuring" in his essay "Of Vaine Subtilties, or Subtill Devices," would surely apply:

> There are certaine frivolous and vaine inventions, or as some call them subtilties of wit, by meanes of which, some men doe often endeavour to get credit and reputation: . . . we see Egges, Wings, Hatchets, Crosses, Globes, Columnes . . . with the measure and proportion of their verses, spreading, lengthening, and shortening them, in such sort as they justly represent such and such a figure. . . . It is a wonderfull testimonie of our judgments imbecilitie, that it should commend and allow of things, either for their rarenesse or noveltie, or for their difficultie, though neither goodnesse or profit be joyned unto them.[7]

But Williams's visual text usually functions in anything but a figurative or emblematic way. He was, in fact, quick to point out that the poem's design need not be emblematic. Rather, it can function "like some kinds of modern painting" in which one "does not necessarily have to paint a photographic representation of his subject."[8] Asked in 1961 whether one of the things he accomplished in his poetry was to "abstract the elements of a work . . . in a way that indicates what seems . . . to be somehow the essential principle of design," Williams replied: "Very definitely. . . . The design of the painting and of the poem I've attempted to fuse. To make it the same thing. And sometimes I don't want to say anything. I just want to present it . . . I don't care if it's representational or not. But to give a design. A design in the poem and a design in the picture should make them more or less the same thing."[9]

Williams's surprising desire to give up the priority of the poem's *saying,* his willingness to admit that "sometimes I don't want to say anything," represents a radical alternative to that tradition in Western poetics, first fully articulated by Plato, which claims everything for the *saying.*[10] It seems a gloss to the moment in *Paterson,* Book Five, when he proclaims:

> Pollock's blobs of paint squeezed out
> with design!
> pure from the tube. Nothing else
> is real   .   .
>
> (*P,* 213)

This is a celebration of painting's plasticity, a renewal in contemporary terms of the Hartpence story which he often told audiences in the late 1940s and early 1950s:

Alanson Hartpence was employed at the Daniel Gallery. One day, the proprietor being out, Hartpence was in charge. In walked one of their most important customers, a woman in her fifties who was much interested in some picture whose identity I may at one time have known. She liked it, and seemed about to make the purchase, walked away from it, approached it and said, finally, "But Mr. Hartpence, what is all that down in this left hand lower corner?"

>   Hartpence came up close and carefully inspected the area men-
>   tioned. Then, after further consideration, "That, Madam," said
>   he, "is paint." (*A,* 240)

Pollock and Hartpence both celebrate the reality of their material, and Williams's own celebration of the plastic reality of art
is equally an exhortation directed at himself: the lines from
Paterson may as well read, "Williams's groups of words blurted
out/ with design!" Williams must approach his own medium in
the manner of a Pollock, or, even more to the point, in the
manner of a Gertrude Stein, to whose "abstraction" and "route
of the vocables" he also pays tribute in Book Five (*P,* 222). Like
Stein, Williams desires to lift writing "to a plane of almost
abstract design" (*SE,* 119). The formal purity of poetry is achieved
not in its saying—that is, in the phonetic and semantic complex-
ities of verbal utterance—but in its visual shaping. And since the
line's shaping is plastic—that is, the result of a manipulation
performed by the eye and not the ear—then its original "source,"
as Charles Olson had outlined it in "Projective Verse," the idea
of its "origin" in the fictive "laws of breath" (see *A,* 329–32), is
annulled. The poem's shape conforms to an arbitrary and a
priori visual patterning.

I am suggesting not only that Williams does not subscribe to
the kind of naive notion of organic unity which leads to the
poem's formal *picturing* of its subject matter, but also that he
comes to reject a more sophisticated organicist formalism which
insists, in Murray Krieger's words, that "whatever the poet at
first mechanically imposes . . . whatever form . . . is given from
the outside must, through transformations within the poem, be
seen to be growing inevitably from within."[11] Krieger is speaking
of meter and rhyme—the kind of "mechanical regularity" of
which Coleridge complained—but it was precisely in order to
justify as "inevitable" and organic the mechanically staggered
arrangement of his variable foot that Williams had turned to
Olson's "Projective Verse." As early as his 1936 essay, "How to
Write," Williams had spoken of discovering the inherent "rules"
of the poem, rules which he thought might govern "the personality speaking, the middle brain, the nerves, the glands, the very
muscles and bones of the body itself speaking."[12] It was to this

notion of "the speaking body" that Olson appealed: "The line comes (I swear it) from the breath, from the breathing of the man who writes, at the moment that he writes, and thus is, it is here that, the daily work, the WORK, gets in, for only he, the man who writes, can declare, at every moment, the line, its metric, and its ending—where its breathings shall come to, termination. . . . the HEART, by way of the BREATH, to the LINE" (*A*, 331). Here the poem's *form* is intimately and organically tied to its *saying*. That is, the length of its line is a function of the unit—the length—of the speaking breath. For all practical purposes, this *generally* means that each line of Williams's variable foot is syntactically bounded. The length of each line is determined by the length of the syntactical unit or units it contains. Consider, for instance, these lines from the "Tribute to the Painters" section of *Paterson*, Book Five:

> The neat figures of
> Paul Klee
> fill the canvas
> but that
> is not the work
> of a child
> the cure began, perhaps
> with the abstraction
> of Arabic art
> (*P*, 222)

All of the lines break at normal syntactic divisions, *except the first*— "of/ Paul Klee"—which breaks in marked contrast to the later prepositional phrases "of a child," "with the abstraction," and "of Arabic art." As Williams began more and more to understand the visual basis of his art, he also began more and more to violate the syntactic integrity of his lines, so that by the time of *Pictures from Brueghel* the syntactic unity of the line seems to interest him not at all. The kind of "hard" enjambment which we witness in the first two lines ("of/ Paul Klee") becomes the rule, not the exception.[13] As a result, the integrity of the line seems to depend upon neither syntax nor breath (usually the two are synonymous anyway), but upon some other principle at odds with both syntax and breath.

Consider the middle stanzas of "The Hunters in the Snow" from the *Pictures* sequence:

> from the left
> sturdy hunters lead in
>
> their pack the inn-sign
> hanging from a
> broken hinge is a stag a crucifix
>
> between his antlers the cold
> inn yard is
> deserted but for a huge bonfire
>
> that flares wind-driven tended by
> women who cluster
> about it to the right beyond
>
> the hill is a pattern of skaters
>
> (PB, 5)

Quite clearly Williams's lines here are organized on the basis of some principle other than syntax or breath. The impulse to breathe occurs more often in midline than at line end. And, to be read aloud, the poem requires that its reader supply certain syntactic pauses which Williams simply does not provide. Williams's lack of punctuation creates, in fact, a visual continuity which defies syntactic closure—at least it makes the reader wary of closure. The most interesting instance of this occurs in the next-to-last line of the quotation, where the prepositional phrase "to the right" can either end the preceding sentence or initiate the next: either the fire is "tended by/ women who cluster/ about it to the right," or, alternately, "to the right beyond/ the hill, is a pattern of skaters." Because there are no syntactic markers, the phrase functions as a kind of visual pun. By reading aloud with a slight hesitation both before and after "to the right," this ambiguity can be rendered orally, but the ambiguity originates in the visual dimension of the poem, in its lack of syntactic markers.

The poem, then, must first be *seen* on the page in order to be fully appreciated as it is read either silently or aloud. Williams's gradual awakening to the visual dimension of his poetry accounts, I think, for the shift in formal arrangement which occurs between *Journey to Love* (1955), composed entirely of staggered tercets, and the seventy-six poems which make up *Pictures of Brueghel* (1962), of which only two, "The Gift" and "The Turtle," use the staggered three-line sequence. As I pointed out earlier, the nine poems which make up the series entitled "Some Simple Measures in the American Idiom and the Variable Foot" indicate the arbitrariness of Williams's visual patterning. Whereas the staggered tercet poems have few or no stanzaic breaks, the poems in *Pictures* are arranged in distinct stanzas, including couplets, tercets, and quatrains. With only three or four exceptions, every poem in this last volume maintains the same stanzaic pattern throughout, and almost all of them have a uniform instead of a staggered left margin. All of this serves, I think, to reinforce a sense of plastic orderliness in the poetry.[14] But Williams's plastic manipulation of his medium does not end here. When he uses the tercet—as he does in forty-nine of the volume's seventy-six poems—each stanza is designed in one of only four ways, as follows:

1) _____
    _____
    _____

2) _____
    _____
    _____

3) _____
    _____
    _____

4) _____
    _____
    _____

The extent of the uniformity of these patterns is even more evident when we realize that pattern 2 is simply the inverse of pattern 1, and pattern 4 is the mirror image of pattern 3, so it is possible to say that there are essentially only two patterns. Furthermore, these stanzaic patterns are unlike the earlier staggered tercet, which would have to be diagrammed by using arrows to indicate that line length is indeterminate and completely variable:

I do not mean to imply that Williams's lines in *Pictures from Brueghel* are uniform in length. His is a loose structure, not a tight one. But the stanzas can be seen as a kind of uniform grid system into which Williams fits the range and multiplicity of his material.[15] Williams's lines are, to use his own oxymoron, *"relatively* uniform." For example, the poem which opens the *Pictures from Brueghel* sequence proper, "Self-Portrait," consists of seven stanzas, all recognizably of this pattern:

In all five of the manuscript versions of "Self-Portrait" at Yale, the second stanza does not fit into the schematic pattern of the poem as a whole, assuming instead its inverse:

Thus, if the opening two stanzas of an early mansucript version are compared to those of the final printed version, it is evident that Williams revised in order to emphasize the poem's visual consistency and orderliness:

> MS version: A big hand close up blue eyed in a red
>   winter hat between
>   crowding shoulders fills
>
>   the canvas smiling
>   arms folded one big ear the
>   right shows the face

Final version: In a red winter hat blue
eyes smiling
just the head and shoulders

crowded on the canvas
arms folded one
big ear the right showing

Williams is imposing the abstract form on his material here, taking the multiplicity of detail he describes and fitting it into a single arbitrary (a priori) and visual pattern.

III

The history of Williams's visual text begins, then, with an almost accidental revelation of consistent formal design in a poem like "The Red Wheelbarrow," a formal design which seems to realize *Spring and All*'s desire for definition, clarity, and formal "outline," but only as a special instance, the manifestation of an extraordinary insight or inspiration. In the 1930s and 1940s, beginning with the objectivist phase, Williams broadens the visual patterning he achieves in "The Red Wheelbarrow" to include almost every poem from which he is absent as a subjective, first-person force. The only way the artist's presence makes a difference to an external reality is if it imposes order upon it. But in this phase Williams feels no need to introduce a consistent visual pattern to any poem in which the authorial "I" is, at least in part, the subject matter. Then, after he begins "objectively" to record instances of the American idiom in order to reveal the inherent form our speech possesses, he arrives at the concept of the variable foot. Throughout most of the poems in which the variable foot occurs in a visually consistent staggered tercet, Williams is working on the assumption that he has discovered a form which reflects the simultaneity, the antagonistic cooperation, of the abstract and the real, order and chaos. But because the staggered tercet reflects Williams's desire to arrive at some original "breath" which is, to paraphrase Olson, the organic source of all beginnings, it denies a simultaneity of opposites and proposes instead their ideal union. The formal schemes of the *Pictures from Brueghel*, finally, restore Williams's poetic to the heterogeneity upon which it is founded, presenting an abstract visual design which challenges and is challenged by the poem's concrete, aural material.

This visual text—a text we encounter visually as an abstraction before we "read" it for whatever concrete reference it possesses—defines the new poetic space in which Williams's late work consciously operates. But the late work also operates within a second visual dimension, one which not only assumes our experience of the text as a visual design but also takes for its subject matter visual art. In his various "pictures" from Brueghel or his treatment of the unicorn tapestries, Williams defines very precisely what he sees as the function of art. In the heterogeneous modern world—a world marked by difference and divorce—no connection except an *aesthetic* one seems to exist between subject and object. Art exists in order to help us define the terms of this relationship—to borrow Williams's metaphor, the terms of the conversation or dialogue between mind and matter.

Despite its achievement, Williams's late work has been slighted for a number of reasons, not the least of them his choice of subject matter and the formal consistency with which he treats it. Charles Olson complained very early on that *Paterson*, Book Five, abandoned the poem's initial concern for the living: "the tapestry, even if the poet called it 'the living fiction,' was a tapestry—a sewn cloth of flowers."[16] Jerome Mazzaro's very fine study of Williams and cubism, "Dimensionality in Dr. Williams' *Paterson*," concludes by saying that Williams is at his strongest when his form is "unconscious," but when he "uses conscious patterns . . . one cannot help feeling a lessening or diverting of this strength."[17] Williams's tapestry is *not* a "sewn cloth of flowers" but printed words on a page, and that metamorphosis from flowers to cloth to words embodies the very dynamic which Olson feels both poem and tapestry abuse. Furthermore, to demand that Williams allow his form to discover itself in the "unconscious" is to demand that he accept a poetics of organic unity which he rejects.

My sense is that Olson, Mazzaro, and many others misunderstand both the metamorphoses Williams works upon his subject matter and the really daring formal innovation which the poems embody. Instead, they see his last work as something of a retreat. However moving, however lovely, however skillful these poems may be, in apparently looking not toward the future but toward the past, they seem to represent Williams's withdrawal from the front ranks of the avant-garde, his descent into the kind of conservatism, even academicism, that so alienated him from T. S. Eliot. Other notable moderns have suffered this same misunderstanding. In the 1950s and 1960s Picasso executed many re-creations of earlier works—ranging from a series of fifty-eight paintings after Velázquez's *Las Meninas*, to one hundred and fifty drawings and twenty-seven oils re-creating Manet's *Déjeuner sur l'herbe* (itself taken, incidentally, from an engraving by Marcantonio Raimondi after a lost painting by Raphael), and to various oils re-creating such paintings as Ingres's *Raphael and Fornarina* and Delacroix's *Femme d'Algiers*. More recently, Larry Rivers has parodied Rembrandt's *Syndics of the Drapers' Guild*, David's *Napoleon in His Study*, and Emanuel Leutze's *Washington Crossing the Delaware*; Andy Warhol has silkscreened any number of commercial and photographic images, including the *Mona Lisa*; Robert Rauschenberg has incorporated reproductions of paintings by Rubens, Velázquez, and da Vinci into his combine-paintings; and Roy Lichtenstein has translated most of the classic modern paintings from Monet to Cézanne and from Matisse to Picasso into the comic-strip world of the benday dot. The phenomenon of recasting masterpieces has become so widespread, in fact, that in 1978 the Whitney Museum organized a popular exhibition on the practice, recognizing for the first time that "the art-about-art theme" had become "a pervasive ingredient" of American art.[18]

John Anderson, in one of the only serious studies of Picasso's *Meninas* cycle, calls such paintings "a gesture of despair . . . the expression of a collective feeling for the historical exhaustion and vitiation of the means and appliance of art."[19] Artists borrow from other artists for many reasons—and a certain amount of the recent resurgence in blatantly borrowed or "stolen" images in American art can indeed be read as "a gesture of despair." But no matter how we read the gesture, this much is clear:

Williams, Picasso, Rivers, Warhol, Rauschenberg, and Lichten-stein have little interest in the "originality" of their own work, at least insofar as their subject matter is concerned, and in revising the "original" they are undermining its authority. What these works signify is a shift in attitude toward the work of art. It is no longer an object of adoration and contemplation, a static masterpiece charged with a sense and meaning fully knowable to any who would enter its world. Rather, the work of art is now dynamic, never fully knowable in and of itself because it refers beyond itself, both as a mimetic structure, a tool of ref-erence, and as a structure which invites interpretation, the op-eration of producing meaning.

In these terms, whenever Williams's Brueghel poems are praised only for the remarkable descriptive *accuracy* of their detail—that is, whenever he is applauded, as he rightly is, for his ability to "translate" the visual into the verbal—the real achievement of his work is understated, even misunderstood. To quote Ed-ward Said, who has articulated better than anyone the distinc-tion I am trying to make, the tendency has been to read Williams's re-creations in terms of "a set of relationships linked together by familial analogy: father and son, the image, the process of genesis, a story." But they partake instead of a different series of relationships—"the brother, discontinuous concepts, para-genesis, construction":

> The first of these series is dynastic, bound to sources and origins, mimetic. The relationships holding in the second series are com-plementarity and adjacency; instead of a source we have an in-tentional beginning, instead of a story a construction. . . . Most important, the text is transformed from an original object into a produced and producing structure whose laws are dynamic not static, whose materiality is textual not genetic, and whose effect is to multiply memory not to fix it.[2]

The greatest source of confusion about Williams's Brueghel poems lies in our consistent failure to remember that they are not literally pictures. When Williams re-creates Brueghel's *Nativity* in *Paterson*, Book Five, that painting is necessarily

new born!
among the words.

(*P*, 226)

Williams's words impose a new form, a new spatial and material arrangement, upon Brueghel's subject matter. Like his famous "This Is Just to Say," the poem "literally enacts the process of replacing absent objects with words," the plums with a note of apology, the painting with a poem.[21] Williams's "translation" from painting to poem is not an exercise in repetition but a project in re-vision; it is not description, but re-creation.

In the late 1930s Williams had praised Charles Henry Ford's *Garden of Disorder and Other Poems* by saying that his poems "revive the senses" and force us "to re-see, re-hear, re-taste, re-smell, and generally re-value all that it was believed had been seen, heard, smelled, and generally valued."[22] This is essentially the project of the Brueghel poems and the fifth book of *Paterson*. Clearly, Williams desires not to assimilate—to "copy"—what "was," but rather to approach it with fresh eyes. "The imagination has to imitate nature," he wrote to Kenneth Burke in 1951, "not to copy it—as the famous speech in *Hamlet* has led us to believe. There is a world of difference there. The whole dynamic of the art approach is involved, to imitate invokes the verb, to copy invokes nothing but imbecility. It is the very essence of the difference between realism and cubism with everything in favor of the latter."[23] By emphasizing its plastic freedom to manipulate nature, cubism draws attention to the process of making art itself, and Williams, in approaching a painting from Brueghel or a scene from the Cloisters tapestries, consistently turns his description of the work to a consideration of the work's making:

> the old women or the young
> or men or boys wielding their needles
> to put in her green thread correctly
> beside the purple, myrtle beside
> holly and the brown threads beside:
> together as the cartoon has plotted it
> for them.
>
> (*P*, 232)

Williams looks at the works of art which rise out of his tradition in order "to refresh himself/ at the sight direct from the 12th/

century," a sight presented to him not so that he can recapture the past but so that he might be able to imitate the vitality of the makers' activity in the present, and make again:

> They draw him imperiously
> to witness them, make him think
> of bus schedules and how to avoid
> the irreverent
>
> .   .   .   .
>
> in his mind eating .   .
> all together for his purposes
>
> (*P,* 231–32)

There is some question as to what is "imperious" here, the work of art or the poet, but Williams *is* being purposely imperious, so outrageously free with the tapestries that they recall "bus schedules" for him. His point, I take it, is simply to emphasize that the work of art compels his own artistic remaking of it. The original "text"—the painting or the tapestry—exists not so that he can discover its "original" purpose, but so that he may turn it to his own purposes, to his own *designs.*

Twice in *Paterson,* once near the end of Book Four and again at the end of Book Five, Williams quotes his grandmother: "The past is for those who lived in the past" (*P,* 187, 239). Although these admonitions apparently challenge Williams's interest in and use of the past in the poem, Williams is not arguing with his grandmother; rather, he is drawing attention to the fact that he is not living in the past so much as the past is living in him. "There can be no rivalry with the past," he told a Washington University audience in the late 1940s. "The new has as its objective not to equal or surpass what has been done before, only to show that its objectives have never dropped away from those which filled the men and women of past times. They copied no one, the freshness of their composition is one of its outstanding features. In the same way we cannot copy them. To create both of us have been enjoined."[24]

Williams's involvement with the past can in fact be summed up by his famous "antagonistic cooperation" oxymoron, doing the same thing differently. Both times Williams describes Brueghel's

Nativity—in *Paterson,* Book Five, and in the Brueghel sequence
proper—he does so in order to emphasize the lack of *copying*
involved in the re-creative act. He admits that the Brueghel
painting was "copied we'll say/ from the Italian masters/ but
with a difference" (*PB,* 6). What makes the difference is "the
resourceful mind/ that governed the whole" (*PB,* 6), the abstracting mind that designs its subject matter after its own fashion. Thus the authenticity of Brueghel's *Nativity* derives from
the fact that Brueghel sees the child's features as he saw them

> many times no doubt
> among his own kids but not of course
> in this setting
> (*P,* 226)

In a similar revaluation of the "original" scene, Williams says
that the features of the attendant soldiery are like those of "the
more stupid/ German soldiers of the late/ war" (*P,* 226). Even
more to the point is Williams's re-creation of his own re-creation, the fourth poem in the Brueghel sequence which comes
"from the Nativity/ which I have already celebrated" in *Paterson,* Book Five (*PB,* 6). In this second version Williams adds
what the *Paterson* version lacked—the consistent abstract design
of the visually ordered text—and his model is as much his own
earlier poem as the Brueghel painting itself.

The eighth poem in the Brueghel sequence possesses the same
double reference as the fourth. Called "The Wedding Dance in
the Open Air," it begins:

> Disciplined by the artist
> to go round
> & round
> (*PB,* 10)

Although Williams is referring to the discipline which Brueghel
asserts over his subject matter, he is referring as well to the
discipline he achieved in his own much earlier poem, "The Dance":

> In Brueghel's great picture, the Kermess,
> the dancers go round, they go round and
> around, the squeal and the blare and the
> tweedle of bagpipes, a bugle and fiddles

> tipping their bellies (round as the thick-
> sided glasses whose wash they impound)
> their hips and their bellies off balance
> to turn them. Kicking and rolling about
> the Fair Grounds, swinging their butts, those
> shanks must be sound to bear up under such
> rollicking measures, prance as they dance
> in Brueghel's great picture, The Kermess.
>
> (*CLP*, 11)

A great deal has been said about this poem, and I need not reiterate the technical facility—the marvelous interweaving of patterns of sound—which Williams employs in arriving at a circular poetic structure to rival the structure of both dance and painting. What interests me is that Williams should choose to *rewrite* it, to revise its organic structure—its "roundness"—and fit it instead to the arbitrary structure of a Brueghel stanza. In fact, in the Brueghel stanza, the blocklike shape of the tercets seems dramatically opposed to the "roundness" of the poem's subject matter. I emphasize this dissolution of "organic unity" in Williams's formal poetic, of form rising from content, because its dissolution represents Williams's recognition of the *antimimetic* basis of form itself, of the *displacement* his form effects upon his subject matter.

The Brueghel stanza, in fact, helps to create a feeling that the poem is actually made up of a series of displacements, each line displacing and revising what had come before, projecting its own displacement in the lines which follow. This is one effect of the kind of hard enjambment on which Williams relies throughout the late poetry, creating a sense of what John Hollander has tellingly labeled "revisionary disclosure."[25] (And I think Hollander would agree that this phrase can function as a complicated pun—"revision" in the sense of both reassessment and reseeing, "disclosure" in the sense of both bringing to light and not admitting to poetic closure.) Each line forces us to acknowledge, at its terminus, the possibility that the next line will mandate a reassessment of our sense of what we're reading. J. Hillis Miller has remarked on this effect, citing lines such as "of red and" (*CLP*, 56), "It is too old, the" (*CLP*, 45), "but" (*PB*, 44), "flash a" (*PB*, 48), "of the" (*PB*, 50):

In such lines each word, especially the last, stands alone . . . but the reader knows that the last word is part of a grammatical construction and will be completed in the next line. . . . The word reaches out with all its strength toward the other words which are for the moment absent. Conjunctions, prepositions, adjectives, when they come at the end of a line, assume an expressive energy as arrows of force reaching toward other words: "of red and →". . . . Into the white space surrounding the word go a multitude of lines of force, charging that space with the almost tangible presence of various words which might come to complete the central word and appease its tension.[26]

What Miller is saying of the line terminus can be said of poems as a whole, of works of art in general. I think it is fair to say of Williams's Brueghel poems and the tapestry sequence in *Paterson,* Book Five, that they are literally some of the possible words which the artwork projects. They fill in the blank space surrounding the canvas or tapestry; they complete it, appease it. That is, the work of art always calls up its interpretation or, more precisely, its *re-creation.*

This opening toward the audience is, I think, what Williams means to suggest by the lack of terminal punctuation in *Pictures from Brueghel* as a whole. Even on the rare occasion when he does resort to punctuation—as in the curious semi-ellipsis which ends "Hunters in the Snow"—it serves to open rather than to close the poem:

> Brueghel the painter
> concerned with it all has chosen
>
> a winter-struck bush for his
> foreground to
> complete the picture .   .
>
>   (*PB,* 5)

The ellipsis here draws the line *and the poem* out, suggests that there is *more to say.* In this projection the poem formally denies the sense of completion and totality which its actual *saying* claims. Need I add that the ellipsis belongs wholly to the visual realm. Only heard, the poem is closed, finalized; seen, it opens out once again, toward us.

It is this opening, I want to finally suggest, which restores Williams's text to the "living," rescues it from the static masterpiece mentality of the museum of which Olson complained when *Paterson,* Book Five, was first published. Writing of Picasso's re-creations of Velázquez's *Las Meninas,* Michel Leiris has asked, "When he deals thus with a work by an earlier artist is he not treating it as an object that has been integrated into the real world, something that must not be allowed to fossilize but must be helped, so to speak, to fulfill its natural evolution by being given a new lease on life?"[27] In a 1951 review of Nicolas Calas's notoriously eccentric *Illumination of the Significance of Bosch's "The Garden of Delights,"* Williams sees Calas's project in much the same light:

> Calas's presentation is the work of a mind that puts itself on a par with Bosch, as though he too were contemporary and his picture, which before he painted it had its "creation" already extant in his consciousness, were a contemporary phenomenon— as it cannot but be—something alive today. Such a view gives the text new authority. It is no longer an explanation in which the present day attempts to put itself into conditions of the past which it cannot know and so stultifies itself. It is rather an evocation in which the present mind brings the past up to today and makes it work before our eyes. It is an eye cast into Bosch's mind, true enough, but it is also our eyes and mind which we lend to the past that it may live again as we watch it performing, alive before us. . . . It makes Bosch come alive and though we can't always be sure (the process would defeat itself if this were true) by releasing itself unrestrainedly it achieves a new insight. (*RI,* 192)

Bosch's work achieves "a new insight" by virtue of its contemporary context. Art lives, in short, through its interpretation, through the re-creation it provokes at the hands of a Calas or a Williams. The poem is a "machine made of words" (*CLP,* 4), to borrow Williams's famous metaphor, and what it produces is interpretation itself.[28]

As Northrop Frye has recently pointed out, the archetype of all re-creative activity is the Bible, "where the New Testament's conception of the Old is, from the point of view of Judaism, a

preposterous and perverse misunderstanding."[29] In turn, and in
the terms Williams employs in *Paterson*, Book Five, the unicorn
tapestry represents something of "a preposterous and perverse"
retelling of the New Testament, a mythological and heretical
secularization of the Christian story. But it is precisely the power
of a story to generate such retellings that attracts Williams. Art,
at its best, invites its own metamorphoses, seeks the voice that
will re-create it not in its own terms but in terms of "the present
mind." It is this re-creating voice of which Williams surely dreamed
when he wrote to Allen Ginsberg on February 27, 1952: "You
shall be the *center* of my new poem of which I shall tell you:
the extension of *Paterson*."[30] Williams's whole work, he claims
in that fifth book which he promised Ginsberg, has been dedicated to

> living and writing
> > answering
> letters
>
> > .   .   .
>
> > and trying
> to get the young
> > to foreshorten
> their errors in the use of words which
> he had found so difficult, the errors
> he had made in the use of the
> poetic line
> > (*P*, 230–31)

Or, as he says a little earlier, in the central lyric addressed to a
nameless woman he has seen on the street: "have you read
anything that I have written?/ It is all for you" (*P*, 220). *Paterson*
is a kind of "letter" addressed especially to a younger generation
of poets like Ginsberg, but to the nameless mass of us as well.
Its culmination lies not in itself, but in us all, its audience.

In *A New World Naked*, Paul Mariani points out that one of
the last-minute changes in *Paterson*, Book Five, involved "the
simple substitution" of the letter from Edward Dahlberg (*P*,
229–30) for one from Cid Corman concerning poetics. Thus,
Mariani argues, "Williams moved the poem away from the sub-

ject of the transmission of the craft to one's sons to the more fundamental issue of the Woman: the hidden core of his poem finally revealing herself."[31] But I think it is fair to argue that the so-called issue of the Woman and the subject of the transmission of the craft are really one and the same. The poem, Williams says, is no more than a "'passionate letter'/ to a woman" (P, 230)—no more, that is, and no less. It is an opening out to "the Woman" and to poetic sons equally. The woman in the Dahlberg letter is meant to recall and echo Marcia Nardi's predicament and the risk she had taken in addressing Williams so intimately. This is the risk Williams's poem has assumed as well. It is no easy thing to let one's work go, to will it away to the possibly preposterous and perverse readings of succeeding generations of readers. By arguing, in fact, that Williams's variable foot is based on a visual sense of poetic form, I have been trying to suggest that most contemporary American poets have, in their efforts to "hear" it, misread it. I suppose I have even been suggesting that Williams mostly misread his own formal accomplishment. He certainly knew it was open to interpretation. "I shrink to take responsibility for what the unskilled students . . . will do with this line," Williams wrote to Robert Creeley, "but I don't for the life of me see how they can escape attempting it."[32] Charles Altieri has suggested that Williams counters or foils the sense of loss and displacement which an opening to interpretation can engender by seeing the poem as a way "of taking up stances towards the world," as "a type for our capacity to act and to be understood."[33] According to Altieri, poetic texts are performances which we must attend to "not simply as the products of acts but as the embodiment of qualities of acting"— precisely Williams's point in emphasizing poetry-making particularly and artistic re-creation generally.[34] In imitating Brueghel he is imitating not so much the subject matter of Brueghel's paintings as the very quality of Brueghel's action. "With action as our center," as Altieri says, "even the simplest themes can provide place and play for the most intense energies."[35] That is, Williams's art is a type for our capacity to act and to be understood *aesthetically.* Williams wants his art to generate more art, just as Brueghel and the unknown weavers of the tapestries have

generated Williams's. This is the full implication of Williams's
visual text: a text which needs us in order to fulfill itself. Needing
more than our hearing of it, it needs, in fact, our *seeing* of it, so
that its form might be apprehended. It requires our response so
that the metamorphoses it projects might begin to be achieved
again and again.

The visual text, finally, defines a way for us all to approach
the world. Williams chooses to re-create works of art in his last
poems because he knows that we accept the idea of the work of
art as an eloquent object, with its eloquence only realized in the
act of perception. In our perception the work of art assumes its
aesthetic status. Williams, I think, approaches the world at large
in these same terms. Like a vast museum, the world too contains
an array of objects which realize their own eloquence insofar as
we *see* them, confront them in an aesthetic sense, even re-create
them. When Williams sees his wife take a bath, he makes of her
a "Portrait of a Woman at Her Bath":

> it is a satisfaction
> a joy
> to have one of those
> in the house
>
> when she takes a bath
> she unclothes
> herself she is no
> Venus
>
> I laugh at her
> an Inca
> shivering at the well
> the sun is
>
> glad of a fellow to
> marvel at
> the birds and the flowers
> look on
> (*PB*, 46)

His wife is made into art, lifted into art's "marvel" by this re-
creative gesture. Likewise, "3 carefully coiffured/ and perfumed
old men" are seen as "a cartoon by Daumier" (*PB*, 41), and a

girl named "Erica" becomes a "melody line" (*PB*, 18). Williams approaches the entire world in an aesthetic light. His visual text compels us to do the same.

NOTES

1. *Poetry* 81 (October 1952): 89–90.

2. *Paterson, Book V: The River of Heaven* is the working title for all of the early drafts of "Asphodel" in the Yale MS quoted below.

3. Williams, "The Art of Poetry," p. 127.

4. The quotation here is probably from Louis Aragon's poem "Les Réalités," in *Le Paysan de Paris* (Paris: Gallimard, 1926), pp. 68–69. Williams socialized with Aragon on his trip to Paris in 1924 (see *A*, 194, 211). If he did not know *Le Paysan* directly, he was probably familiar with Robert Sage's review of the book, "La Réalité," *transition* 2 (May 1927): 160–63. Sage takes Aragon's poem for his epigraph and notes as well that it underscores Aragon's desire to treat words as things, constructed of syllables, "no less real than a brick house" (p. 161). Williams's poem "The Dead Baby" appeared in this particular number of *transition,* as did the reproduction of Juan Gris's *Dish of Pears* discussed earlier.

5. The only major exception is his treatment of Brueghel's *Adoration of the Magi* at the outset of Part Three, where he adopts the verse paragraph format characteristic of many poems written in the late 1940s such as "Two Pendants." This can be explained, I think, as a strategic necessity, designed to heighten our sense of the formal accomplishment that the staggered tercet embodies in the long tapestry sequence which culminates Book Three.

6. Miller, *Poets of Reality,* p. 301.

7. Montaigne, *Essays,* trans. John Florio (New York: Dutton, 1910), I, 351–52.

8. Quoted in John C. Thirlwall, "William Carlos Williams' *Paterson:* The Search for a Redeeming Language—A Personal Epic in Five Parts," *New Directions 17* (New York: New Directions, 1961), p. 289.

9. Walter Sutton, "A Visit with William Carlos Williams," *Minnesota Review* 1 (Spring 1961): 321–22.

10. See, for instance, Plato's *Phaedrus,* where speech is privileged over writing because, for Plato, meaning is only present at the moment of an utterance's production. The pervasive influence on Western poetics and metaphysics of Plato's point of view has been one of Jacques Derrida's favorite subjects. I have examined some aspects of its influence upon contemporary American poetry in my "David Antin and the Oral Poetics Movement," *Contemporary Literature* 23 (Autumn 1982): 428–50.

11. Murray Krieger, *Theory of Criticism: A Tradition and Its System* (Baltimore: Johns Hopkins University Press, 1976), p. 119.

12. Reprinted in *Interviews with William Carlos Williams: "Speaking Straight Ahead,"* ed. Linda Welshimer Wagner (New York: New Directions, 1976), p. 98.

13. The term is from Hollander, *Vision and Resonance,* pp. 99–101.

14. Joel Conarroe has stressed the plastic orderliness of the Brueghel poems in "The Measured Dance: Williams' 'Pictures from Brueghel,'" *Journal of Modern Literature* 1 (May 1971): 565–77, yet I do not believe he quite recognizes the vigor of Williams's design in these poems, the extent of his plastic manipulation of the words.

15. My phrasing here is again indebted to Lawrence Alloway, who speaks of the loose structure of the grid-system in describing the combine-paintings of Robert Rauschenberg. Alloway suggests that grid organization is the primary compositional device utilized by any artist who accepts an aesthetics of heterogeneity; see Alloway, *Robert Rauschenberg,* p. 5. A fuller and more suggestive discussion of the grid can be found in Rosalind Krauss's introductory essay to the catalogue for an exhibition at the Pace Gallery, December 16, 1978–January 20, 1979, *Grids: Format and Image in 20th Century Art* (New York: Pace Gallery, 1980). In a way particularly relevant to my conception of Williams's aesthetics, Krauss comments on the manner in which the grid functions in modern art: "In the overall regularity of its organization, it is the result not of imitation, but of aesthetic decree. Insofar as its order is that of pure relationship, the grid is a way of abrogating the claims of natural objects to have an order particular to themselves."

16. Charles Olson, *"Paterson* (Book Five)," *Evergreen Review* 3 (Summer 1959): 220.

17. Jerome Mazzaro, "Dimensionality in Dr. Williams' *Paterson,"* *Modern Poetry Studies* 1 (1970): 117.

18. Jean Lipman and Richard Marshall, *Art About Art* (New York: Dutton, 1978), p. 6.

19. John Anderson, "Faustus/Velázquez/Picasso," in *Picasso in Perspective,* ed. Gert Schiff (Englewood Cliffs, N.J.: Prentice-Hall, 1976), pp. 158, 161.

20. Edward Said, *Beginnings: Intention and Method* (New York: Basic Books, 1975), pp. 66–67.

21. Altieri, "Presence and Reference," p. 499.

22. William Carlos Williams, introduction to Charles Henry Ford, *The Garden of Disorder and Other Poems* (London: Europa, 1938), p. 9.

23. Letter of 24 January 1951, quoted in Mariani, *A New World Naked,* p. 633.

24. Williams, "A Cry in the Night," Yale MS.

25. Hollander, *Vision and Resonance,* p. 111.

26. Miller, *Poets of Reality*, p. 299–300.

27. Michel Leiris, "Picasso and the Human Comedy, or the Avatars of Fat-Foot," trans. Stuart Gilbert, in *Picasso in Perspective*, p. 145.

28. The language here—and the general drift of my argument—owes much to Gilles Deleuze, "Antilogos, or the Literary Machine," in *Proust and Signs,* trans. Richard Howard (New York: Braziller, 1974), especially pp. 128–36.

29. Northrop Frye, "The Meaning of Recreation: Humanism in Society," *Iowa Review* ll (Winter 1980): 7. For a somewhat fuller treatment see Frye's short book *Creation & Recreation* (Toronto: University of Toronto Press, 1980).

30. Quoted in Emily Wallace, *A Bibliography of William Carlos Williams*, p. 95.

31. Mariani, *A New World Naked*, p. 707.

32. Quoted in Mariani, "Creeley and Williams," p. 185.

33. Altieri, "Presence and Reference," pp. 492, 509.

34. Altieri, *Act and Quality*, p. 181.

35. Ibid., p. 236.

INDEX

Note on the Author

Henry M. Sayre was born and raised in Boulder, Colorado. He has taught American literature at both Wake Forest University and the University of Washington and currently teaches art history at Oregon State University. He was awarded an NEH Fellowship for 1983–84 to study performance art in the 1970s.

DATE DUE

DEMCO 38-297